DEVIL'S ADVOCATES

DEVIL'S ADVOCATES is a series of books devoted to exploring the classics of horror cinema. Contributors to the series come from the fields of teaching, academia, journalism and fiction, but all have one thing in common: a passion for the horror film and a desire to share it with the widest possible audience.

'The admirable Devil's Advocates series is not only essential – and fun – reading for the serious horror fan but should be set texts on any genre course.'
Dr Ian Hunter, Professor of Film Studies, De Montfort University, Leicester

'Auteur Publishing's new Devil's Advocates critiques on individual titles... offer bracingly fresh perspectives from passionate writers. The series will perfectly complement the BFI archive volumes.' Christopher Fowler, *Independent on Sunday*

'Devil's Advocates has proven itself more than capable of producing impassioned, intelligent analyses of genre cinema... quickly becoming the go-to guys for intelligent, easily digestible film criticism.' *Horror Talk.com*

'Auteur Publishing continue the good work of giving serious critical attention to significant horror films.' *Black Static*

 DevilsAdvocatesbooks

DevilsAdBooks

DEVIL'S ADVOCATES

HOUSE OF USHER

EVERT JAN VAN LEEUWEN

auteur

Acknowledgments

I would like to thank the staff at Auteur Publishing for their hard work in putting this Devil's Advocates volume together. This little book is for my colleague and friend Michael Newton: thanks for the inspiring film discussions and moral support.

First published in 2019 by
Auteur, 24 Hartwell Crescent, Leighton Buzzard LU7 1NP
www.auteur.co.uk
Copyright © Auteur 2019

Series design: Nikki Hamlett at Cassels Design
Set by Cassels Design www.casselsdesign.co.uk

British Library Cataloguing-in-Publication Data
A catalogue record for this book is available from the British Library

ISBN paperback: 978-1-911325-60-4
ISBN ebook: 978-1-911325-61-1

CONTENTS

INTRODUCTION: DISCOVERING *USHER*

On 14 May 1990, at 22:00 (Dutch time), the BBC aired the first episode of *The Curse of Corman*. This TV series introduced American International's Poe pictures to a new generation. It was then that I discovered *House of Usher* (1960). For some strange reason I was enthralled from the opening sequence of the film. There was something irresistibly alluring about this picture. At the time I could describe the film only as bizarre, like nothing I'd seen before. I now understand that watching it was (and still is) an immersive aesthetic experience that works on an emotional, rather than an intellectual level. The opening sequence creates a wonderfully mysterious mood that is sustained throughout the film by the intensely gothic *mise-en-scène* and romantic music. I was thrilled by the charismatic eccentricity of Vincent Price's Roderick and above all by the alternating mellifluous and melancholy tones of his voice. Teenagers of a certain cast can empathise with Roderick's angst-ridden personality.

The films that followed in the series all featured bewildered sufferers, victims of unnameable, or unknowable terrors of the mind. This made them more intense, if less shocking, than most of the horror fantasies I had encountered at the cinema so far. It never occurred to me that *House of Usher* was a horror picture; it was fascinating, gripping, but not scary. I studied the credits to find out who did what, discovering the individual talents of Poe, Matheson, Corman, and later Burt Shonberg, along the way. I had not been much of a reader at school, but after *The Curse of Corman* struck I requested and received a volume of Poe stories from my parents, and developed a love affair with all things gothic, horror and science fiction, from Nathaniel Hawthorne to Clifford Simak. I also started collecting AIP films on VHS and DVD, becoming an American International evangelist on a mission to convert my friends to the church of Corman and co.

Thirty years earlier, a magazine advertisement had announced 'the most important picture in the history of American International': *House of Usher*. The advert's centrepiece is a cross-sectional view of a coffin, inhabited by a curvaceous woman wearing a diaphanous gown. Her wide-eyed gasp expresses the terror that the claustrophobic image is supposed to evoke in the mind of the beholder. The

Fig. 1 Photograph of advertisement (from author's own collection)

predominantly dark hews and the zig-zag downward trajectory of the vertical graphics suggest that this picture will take the audience on a journey into the macabre nether regions below the 'ungodly … the evil House of Usher'. By foregrounding the wide-screen, colour format of the film, this trade ad also appealed to fans of Hammer's lusciously photographed and equally coffin-adorned *The Curse of Frankenstein* (1957) and *Horror of Dracula* (1958). If this failed to convince horror enthusiasts that *House of Usher* was worth the price of admission, the trailer ensured them that this was 'AN AMERICAN INTERNATIONAL MASTERPIECE', a must-see picture for all those youngsters who had been flocking to the drive-ins and hard-tops to see AIP weirdies since 1956.

By announcing their film as the most significant event in the company's history, AIP was taking a commercial risk. From their inception as the American Releasing Corporation in 1954, they had been successful with a string of low-budget teen-oriented genre pictures: Westerns, science fiction and melodramas. The brash slogans advertising *House of Usher* could leave audiences disappointed; moreover, it could invite critics to go on a 78 minute fault-finding mission. But, as usual with AIP, their gamble paid off. Audiences came in droves and reviewers were full of praise. *The Hollywood Reporter* called it 'a class horror picture' (qtd in Williams 164). *Variety* considered it a 'striking elaboration on Poe's short story … mounted with care, skill and flair. The *New York Herald Tribune* praised the way AIP had successfully adapted Poe's peculiar style for the screen and concluded that the film marked 'a restoration of finesse and craftsmanship to the genre of dread' (qtd in Frank 91). The passage of time has only enhanced *House of Usher*'s status as a landmark film. In 2005, America's National Film Preservation Board included the picture in its registry of films to be preserved.

Today's younger movie audiences have more difficulty watching the film. I have screened it for various groups of students, including MA students of the gothic. Most have giggled and laughed for the duration of the film, finding themselves quite incapable of taking it seriously. To be sure, they enjoy it, but mostly for what they consider its camp style, over-the-top acting and dated effects. A one-star customer review of a DVD release of *House of Usher* sums up the film's ambivalent appeal in the twenty-first century. According to this Amazon shopper, *House of Usher* 'is an odd film. It's comparatively short (just one and a quarter hours) yet can seem considerably longer'; it has 'a meagre cast with very little happening for most of its duration'. The reviewer was equally unimpressed with the film's horror elements: 'the house interior for me was just not "creepy" enough'. Yet despite these drawbacks, the reviewer confesses that 'this is a movie for some reason I watch time and time again – not sure why though'.

According to the best-selling horror novelist Stephen King it was the 'hallucinatory eeriness' of AIP's Poe pictures 'that made them special' (2000: 28). King has 'never forgotten the corpse's close-up', in *Pit and the Pendulum* (1961), 'shot through a red filter and a distorting lens which elongated the face into a huge silent scream' (2000: 29). While King here conflates two separate scenes from the film, he was clearly struck by the expressionistic aesthetics of the picture, the way in which the composition of the frames, as well as the shape and colour of the images, were deliberately distorted to achieve strong and lasting emotional effects.

It is this emotional intensity conveyed through the *mise-en-scène* that sets the Poe pictures apart from their immediate rivals. The Poe pictures appealed to AIP's target audience – teenagers – because their aesthetics were also akin to the look and feel of ECs horror comics, like *Tales from the Crypt* and *Vault of Horror*.

In their atmosphere they echoed the dread of impending doom expressed in earlier AIP films like *The Day the World Ended* (1955) and *Not of this Earth* (1956). More than any of the other Poe pictures, *House of Usher* is a work of pulp expressionism that appeals to the angst holed up inside the minds of many a teenage audience member. Like a magic lantern, the film projector reveals a series of beautifully crafted, colourful tableau that in sequence give expression to Poe's vision of human frailty and corruption, and the void that awaits beyond the threshold of life.

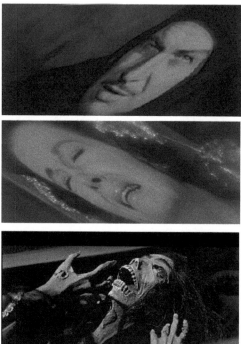

Figs. 2–4 Image distortion

This instalment of Auteur's Devil's Advocates series explains why *House of Usher* has attracted a cult audience for nearly 60 years. In chapter one, the juxtaposition of Poe's and Corman's artistic theory and artistic method shines a light on the creative synergy of their collaboration. The structural analysis of Poe's story and Richard Matheson's script, in chapter two, highlights the films fidelity to Poe's original, despite major alterations in characterisation and plot. Chapter three shows how Corman's crew amalgamated Poe's dark Romantic aesthetics with more expressionistic techniques to create an atmosphere of existential dread with a timeless affective quality. Chapter four discusses the Usher siblings as rebels without a chance, caught in a futile struggle to free themselves from their ancestral yoke. I hope these chapters will give you some indication of the pleasure, sense of wonder and food for thought *House of Usher* has given me over the past decades, and how it can still be a meaningful picture in the twenty-first century.

CHAPTER 1: THE SEEDS OF *USHER*: OF DEATH AND THE MUSE

At high school, Roger Corman wrote an essay on 'The Fall of the House of Usher', became a fan of Poe, and subsequently received a volume of his works for Christmas (BFI 2013). As a teenager Corman also read magazines like *Astounding Science Fiction* (Naha 1982: 5). By reading Poe and the pulps simultaneously, Corman must have realised that the nineteenth-century author's brand of dark Romanticism, with its emphasis on psychological rather than visceral horror, looked forward to the type of post-gothic horror and science fiction published in *Weird Tales* and *Amazing Stories*. In fact, by being reprinted in these magazines, Poe's tales and poems found a whole new audience in the twentieth century. During Corman's teenage years, Poe's immediate heirs were H.P. Lovecraft, Clark Ashton Smith and Ray Bradbury, masters of the short story form and unsurpassed – since Poe – at creating a melancholy, brooding atmosphere, suffused with a sense of impending revelation or doom that pervaded a plot in which tension increases throughout only to withhold a full expression of the discovery. The refusal to fully reveal the monster, or dispel the mystery, allows the reader to continue the creative exploration of the philosophical idea or social theme explored in the story. This is what speculative horror and science fiction is all about: activating intellectual curiosity. Corman has stated that he 'particularly … enjoys the speculative aspects' (Garris 2014) of science fiction. By describing Poe as an author who 'probed the farthest reaches of the mind' (BFI 2013), Corman reveals an understanding of him as a speculative writer, a creative explorer of unknown regions and experiences, not in the future, the past, or outer-space, but as Poe himself defined it in his poem 'Dream-Land': 'Out of Space – out of Time' (*Complete Poems*, 2000: 344), inside the human psyche.

Poe and Corman share more than an interest in the unconscious; as Pawel Aleksandrowicz points out: 'both … are preoccupied with death' (2016: 154). More specifically, I would argue, Poe and Corman are existential artists, fascinated by the theme of death not as a source of outright horror – to shock an audience with graphic portrayals of murder and mayhem – but as a trope through which to explore questions concerning the meaning and purpose of individual as well as collective human lives. Poe expressed this most succinctly in his poem 'The Conqueror Worm' in which he likened mankind to a set of 'Mimes' in a 'motley drama' of which 'much Madness, and more Sin, / And Horror' are 'the soul of the plot'. In this play, mankind is controlled by 'vast formless things' only to fall prey to 'A blood-red thing' that devours them all (*Complete Poems* 2000: 325-6). That Corman also reflected on the meaning of human lives and the ethics of human thought and behaviour in his art becomes apparent by his inclusion of the voice of God, in the opening sequence of *Attack of the Crab Monsters* (1956), who thunders over an ominous sky: 'And the Lord said, I will destroy man whom I have created from the face of the earth; both man, and beast, and the creeping thing, and the fowls of the air; for it repenteth me that I have made them' (Genesis 6:7). While the giant *papier-mâché* crabs in the film will struggle to scare a ten-year old, the biblical epigraph at the outset creates an apocalyptic tone that is sustained throughout the picture by the desolate landscape and claustrophobic action, leaving the Atomic-Age audience pondering the efficacy of nuclear science. While it may be tempting to call Poe a poor man's Percy Shelley and Corman a cheapskate Jack Arnold, I prefer to call them both producers of the thinking person's fantastic fiction.

POE'S MORIBUND POETICS

In Poe's day, graveyard poetry, gothic novels and supernatural verse narratives were very much in vogue. Some of the most successful productions in these genres – Young's *Night Thoughts*, Radcliffe's *Mysteries of Udolpho*, Byron's *Manfred*, Coleridge's 'Ancient Mariner' and Mary Shelley's *Frankenstein* – have become literary classics. Poe's art belongs firmly in this darker Romantic literary tradition. Next to being a poet and storyteller, Poe was also an editor at some of the most successful magazines of the day – *The Southern Literary Messenger*, *Burton's Gentleman's Magazine*, *Graham's* – and contributed to fashionable publications like *Godey's Lady's Book*. Yet he found it difficult to fulfil an editorial position for any length of time, quarrelling endlessly with his literary peers and making enemies along the way. Poe tried (and failed) several times to set up a literary magazine that in his eyes would raise the standard of American letters. This shows that the antebellum author had serious critical as well as artistic ambitions. He was not averse to popularity, fame, or even infamy (see Quinn 1998; Silverman 1991).

Throughout his career Poe worked hard at his job, frequently revising his poems and

stories to achieve the aesthetic perfection he sought, even if he devoted his talents
to an industry that was focused on exploiting literary fashions and current topics of
debate, rather than promoting original art. During his brief career Poe mastered the
conventions of Byronic, gothic and sentimental fiction to such a degree that he could
produce straightforward as well as parodic stories and poems in these popular styles.
He produced satires, burlesques and non-fiction essays on a remarkably diverse range
of topics from polar exploration to landscape gardening and the gold rush. In 1844, he
hoaxed many New Yorkers with a mock article on a transatlantic balloon flight. Poe
also responded to the widespread popularity of mesmerism by publishing 'Mesmeric
Revelation' (1844) and 'The Facts in the Case of M. Valdemar' (1845). Some readers
took these pieces as true stories, but Poe described 'Valdemar' as a hoax to a friend
(Ostrom 1948v2: 337) and explained to the public that what they had taken for a
revelation was in fact a fiction (*Essays and Reviews* (herewith ER) 1984: 1367). Poe also
tried his hand at a lengthier popular genre: the serialised adventure novel, but aborted
both narratives (*Rodman* and *Pym*) before completion. The extent to which Poe was
willing to compromise his own artistic ideals in order to get published and paid had its
limits.

In his most successful tales and poems – 'The Lake' (1827), 'The Doomed City' (1831),
'Shadow – A Parable' (1835), 'Ligeia' (1838), 'The Fall of the House of Usher' (1839),
'The Masque of the Red Death' (1842), 'Dream-Land' (1844) and 'The Raven' (1845) –
Poe was able to finely balance his aesthetic principles, the themes that fascinated him
personally, and the demands of the commercial publishing industry. In these productions
Poe achieved what he called 'Supernal Beauty', an otherworldly, ethereal quality that
produces *an elevating excitement of the Soul*' (ER 1984: 92-3). While there is little direct
evidence of how readers responded to Poe's work in his day, the enthusiastic response
to 'The Raven' suggests that his art indeed had the potential to elevate reader's souls.
Poe had written this poem 'for the express purpose of running – just as [he] did the
"Gold-Bug"' (Ostrom 1948v2: 287). Despite being a commercial composition, drenched
in the brooding melancholy of the dark Romantic school and containing enough hints of
morbid mysteries to please readers hooked on the gothic, 'The Raven' also effused an
otherworldly quality that fascinated readers and auditors alike. A commentator on one
of Poe's public performances of the poem described the poet as a spellbinder (see Van

Leeuwen 2016: 45). Indeed, the mesmeric power of Poe's art lies in its unique aesthetics, not in its subject matter, which is often cliché and sometimes 'borrowed' from previously published sources. It is through the forms, colours and sounds that together constitute the imagery and tone of his best tales and poems that Poe achieves his paradoxical mood of soul-elevating terror.

In April 1846, after 'The Raven' had made Poe a literary lion in New York, the author revealed how he managed to achieve the Supernal Beauty that had entranced his readers and audiences. In 'The Philosophy of Composition', he argued that great literary compositions are not the result of 'fine frenzy' or 'ecstatic intuition' but of 'step by step' planning and 'precision' in execution (ER 1984: 14-15). It is the writer's command over his artistic medium and his masterful compositional skills that give him the power to control a reader's or auditor's response to the text. Poe points out that his insight into the meaning and suggestiveness of words, phrases, rhythms and sounds allowed him to conjure the fitting mood for his chosen subject. He concludes that his insertion of a single metaphorical phrase in the final stanza of 'The Raven' allowed him to 'dispose the mind [of the reader] to seek a moral in all that has been previously narrated' (ER 1984: 25), turning the bird from a supernatural agent into the emblem of a universal emotion: 'Mournful and Never-ending Remembrance' (ibid.). A good writer, in Poe's eyes, is a good manipulator of the senses, capable of infusing beauty and intellectual excitement into the darkest of themes.

Poe's poetics can be understood as a literary form of chiaroscuro, through which the tiniest sparkle of light shines brighter by dint of being enveloped in utter darkness. In turn, the shadows cast by an object will grow more prominent the brighter the light illuminating it. Poe gleaned this aesthetic from the charnel sublimity of graveyard poetry, with its focus on the transience and sorrows of everyday life, the inevitability of decay in nature, and the Christian desire and hope for spiritual transcendence (see Van Leeuwen 2014). Such poetry was still popular in Poe's day. It is no surprise, therefore, that in seeking to earn a living as a poet and magazine writer, and having a personal fascination with themes of death and the afterlife, Poe adapted the conventions of the graveyard school to develop a style of his own that was formally and thematically innovative by dint of the absence of a traditional Christian moral framework and a focus on aesthetic rather than didactic impact.

Rather than being a sign of a diseased mind, Poe's moribund poetics should be judged in the context of his broader artistic philosophy. For Poe, a poem has 'for its *immediate* object, pleasure, not truth' (*ER* 1984: 11) and should be '*universally* appreciable' (*ER* 1984: 16). For Poe 'that pleasure which is at once the most intense, the most elevating, and the most pure, is … found in the contemplation of the beautiful' (ibid.). While Poe wrote of poetry specifically, he acknowledged that this 'Poetic Sentiment … may develop itself in various modes – in Painting, in Sculpture, in Architecture, in the Dance – very especially in Music – and very peculiarly, and with a wide field, in the composition of the Landscape Garden' (*ER* 1984: 77). To achieve the Supernal Beauty that can excite the greatest possible elevation of soul, Poe argued, a writer should first decide on 'a novel' and 'vivid effect' (*ER* 1984: 13). Secondly, he 'should consider whether it can best be wrought by incident or tone – whether by ordinary incidents and peculiar tone, or the converse, or by peculiarity both of incident and tone' (*ER* 1984: 13-4). The overall effect achieved by the balancing of incident and tone should not pertain to total clarity, which Poe associates with cold scientific truth, but should produce 'indefinite sensations' (*ER* 1984: 11). Poe explains himself by means of an example: 'He who regards [a star] directly and intensely sees, it is true, the star, but it is the star without a ray – while he who surveys it less inquisitively is conscious of all for which the star is useful to us below – its brilliancy and its beauty' (*ER* 1984: 8). Supernal Beauty can be achieved only through a level of obscurity – as in Edmund Burke's definition of the sublime – that forces the creative imagination into action as it attempts to complete the image presented suggestively, not as it exists objectively, but as it exists ideally, in the mind of the beholder, together with the associations it carries that excite the soul.

Death, when viewed through the lens of Poe's poetics, is not merely the negation of life, engendering the decay of once living matter. Rather, as the ultimate unknown – escaping even the clutches of the most advanced methods of empirical scientific investigation – death becomes one of the most obscure, and therefore most evocative subjects for the creative imagination, a potent source of 'indefinite sensations', paradoxical mixtures of wonder and awe, fear and hope, longing and loathing. Above all, it is death's power to conjure feelings of sweet melancholy (Byronic romanticism), dreadful fascination (gothic sensationalism) and longing for a spiritual afterlife (graveyard poetry) that makes it a fitting subject for the artist seeking to excite the soul.

In *The Power of Blackness*, Harry Levin describes Poe's work as the art of 'morbid curiosity', of a 'restless desire, to penetrate the ultimate secret' (1958: 85) of what lies beyond the veil. Poe himself speaks of the true poet's 'burning thirst' to discover 'the immortal essence of man's nature' (*ER* 1984: 686), which shows itself in

> a wild effort to reach the beauty above. It is a forethought of the loveliness to come. It is a passion to be satiated by no sublunary sights, or sounds, or sentiments, and the soul thus athirst strives to allay its fever in futile efforts at *creation*. Inspired with a prescient ecstasy of the beauty beyond the grave, it struggles by multiform novelty of combination among the things and thoughts of Time, to anticipate some portion of that loveliness whose very elements, perhaps, appertain solely to Eternity. And the result of such effort, on the part of souls fittingly constituted, is alone what mankind have agreed to denominate Poetry. (ibid.)

Many of Poe's poems and stories detail what Levin calls journeys to the end of night: 'the imaginary voyage becomes a catastrophic quest, a pursuit of exciting knowledge attained at the price of destruction', an 'attempt to push human awareness beyond the grave' (1958: 89). Understandably, the grave becomes the focal point in Poe's art, either as a setting or as a thematic concept. The most novel and paradoxical effects that are most vividly expressed in Poe's art, through its diction, imagery, rhythms and tonal qualities are the fearful beauties of decay and a wonder concerning the nature of the spirit world that awaits. His speakers and protagonists express both a longing for and simultaneous dread of their inevitable encounter with Death. One of Poe's most famous poems, 'Dream-Land', perfectly expresses these paradoxical feelings of sweet melancholy and dreadful curiosity at discovering 'a wild weird clime' that will forever remain mysterious. This is a dark region of the mind where

> ...the traveller meets aghast
> Sheeted Memories of the Past –
> Shrouded forms that start and sigh
> As they pass the wanderer by –
> White-robed forms of friends long given,
> In agony, to the Earth – and Heaven.

But instead of being a scene of pure horror, the speaker reveals that

> For the heart whose woes are legion
> 'Tis a peaceful, soothing region –
> For the spirit that walks in shadow
> O! it is an Eldorado!
> (*Complete Poems* 2000: 344-45)

'The Fall of the House of Usher' contains another of these imaginative 'journeys to the end of night'. But in contrast to some of Poe's more idealistic conceptions of man's spiritual afterlife, this story presents the reader with Roderick Usher's nightmarish realisation that all matter must inevitably decay and that even his soul, inextricably wound up with his body, is not immune to disintegration. It is a story about the fear of death and the awaiting void.

POE'S POSTHUMOUS COLLABORATION WITH CORMAN

Film historian Thomas Doherty explains that American International Pictures 'designed its product line for maximum teen appeal and minimum adult offense' (2002: 127). Topics like hot rod racing, juvenile delinquency, aliens, monsters, sex, drugs and rock 'n' roll were staple ingredients of their films, always handled with care, to excite teenage interest without causing too much controversy. While for any film company turning a profit is a necessary aim in making a movie, Corman explains that as a director he was never in it for the money alone. He had entered the industry because he 'wanted to do something more artistic' than becoming an engineer (qtd in Naha 1982: 5). During his 'year off in Europe' Corman had studied literature at Oxford and lived the bohemian café life in Paris, creating 'film treatments'. Back home he became a script reader and briefly worked as a grip for TV productions (Corman 1998: 15-8). After selling his first story to the movies, and seeing it botched in production, Corman decided to take 'full artistic control' (qtd in Naha 1982: 8) and went into the moviemaking business with *Monster from the Ocean Floor* (1954).

While Corman's films of the 50s are hampered by low production budgets, the director has explained that 'for the most part, I tried to find something worthwhile in every project and bring that element to the surface ... I tried to put a little of myself into each' film (qtd in Naha 1982: 42). Making films was clearly a means for Corman to express himself and to explore themes that he cared about, from unusual angles. For instance, Corman explains that Lou Russoff's screenplay for *Apache Woman* (1955) 'was a good action script', but he 'added a subplot dealing with prejudice against ... half-breed' Americans 'trapped between white and Indian culture' (Corman 1998: 30), adding a subtext to the film through which he could voice his critique of a significant socio-political subject.

While the plots of Corman's films are often straightforward, his characters are often more complex. As Aleksandrowicz points out: 'most of his heroes and heroines are in one way or another excluded from the mainstream of society and often in conflict with it' (2016: 140). This focus on the outsider in Corman's films has a biographical context. Corman has explained that he always felt 'more comfortable socially on the fringe with those who didn't run with the in-crowd' (Corman 1998: 3). In his films he was also interested in exploring alternative perspectives of the world. This explains the striking moments of 'gender role reversal' (Aleksandrowicz 2016: 130) in his early Westerns and why in the tongue-in-cheek *Creature from the Haunted Sea* (1961) the monster wins and humanity loses for being just too silly and selfish to cope with reality.

No matter how low his budget and clichéd his script, Corman always thought about how he would tell his story, what his angle was going to be, technically as well as thematically. He explains that from the outset of his career he was 'most concerned with screen images' (qtd in Naha 1982: 94) and that from his first directorial effort, *Five Guns West* (1955), 'the elements of an individual style were taking shape' (Corman 1998: 29). According to Corman, 'some of the definitive elements of [his] style' are 'quirky plots built on somewhat gruesome premises; fast-cutting and fluid camera moves; composition in depth' and 'unconventional, well-sketched characters' (1998: 62). Key terms here are 'quirky', 'gruesome', 'fast', 'fluid' and 'unconventional'. It is these elements that set Corman apart from his rivals. Corman's method foregrounds the aesthetic over the narrative aspects of a movie.

Like Poe's tales of terror, Corman's fantastic films are centred around a specific idea, concept or personality expressed through a carefully developed cinematic style that eschews naturalism for the sake of heightened expression, to pursue the idea, rather than the narrative. In terms of plot structure, his films also resemble the weird fiction of Poe and his heirs. He believed that a low-budget film relied on a 'contained situation' (1998: 27) that minimises the complexity of the plot, which in turn minimizes the number of actors and sets needed to tell the story effectively. His comments on the early science fiction shocker *Day the World Ended* reveal how much belief Corman had in his method: 'we designed that movie for success' (qtd in Naha 1982: 13). Here the director unwittingly echoes Poe's confident claim that he had foreseen the popularity of 'The Raven' because he had designed and executed it 'for the express purpose of running' (Ostrom 1948v1: 287).

Like Poe, Corman also infused his horror and science fiction with a more Romantic quality that foregrounds their mysteriousness over their sensationalism. The prologue to *Not of this Earth*, for instance, invites viewers to activate their creative imagination in order to be taken on a fantastic voyage beyond the limits of empirical reality:

You are about to adventure
into the Dimension of
The Impossible!

To enter this realm
you must set your
mind free from the earthly
fetters that bind it!

If the events you are about
to witness are unbelievable,
it is only because your
Imagination is chained!

Sit back, relax and believe…
So that YOU may cross
the brink of time and space…
into that land you sometimes
visit in your dreams!

This epigraph rephrases Poe's 'Dream-land'. Poe's idea that the creative imagination has the power to see, grasp and believe in what baffles reason and the human senses is here made accessible and understandable to a teenage mind watching moving pictures on a silver screen. Like Poe's ghoulish speculative fictions, Corman's fantastic films invite the viewer to enter a world of dreams that is simultaneously fascinating and frightening, but which for all its macabre trappings and mysteries can be safely explored because it is a realm produced by the artist's creative imagination. The heightened stylisation of the imagery foregrounds the artistic medium through which the artist gives expression to his dark vision, stifling any sense of verisimilitude the picture may contain, but allowing the viewer to experience with the film's protagonists the elevating excitement, as well as the terrors, of the soul engendered by the metaphysical discoveries they make about the fate of humanity.

Understandably, most of Corman's fantastic films of the 50s explore the public's angst in the face of impending nuclear war. But even then, *Day the World Ended* (1955) was more than a low-budget copy of a successful Hollywood formula. Corman saw it also as 'a psychological study of a small group of people thrown together under unusual circumstances' (Corman 1998: 31), not unlike the later and more notorious *Night of the Living Dead* (1968). Set in 1970, during the aftermath of 'Total Destruction Day', the film, like Romero's masterpiece, juxtaposes communalism and individualism, altruism and self-interest in the face of impending and inevitable doom. Above all, and for all its ramshackle production values, the film eschews simple dichotomies of good and evil and invites viewers to reflect on what kind of motivations underlie the characters' hopes, fears and actions, leading potentially to greater understanding of the complexity of the human psyche.

Poe was fascinated with death as a bridge to the spirit world, or a doorway into man's inner-most spirit. His creative imagination produced sometimes wonderful, but often hellish visions of spiritual realms and states of consciousness, expressed by the hopeful, fearful and often lunatic voices that constitute his poetry and fiction. Corman's fascination with death was less ethereal, and his artistic technique was less poetic; but his exploration of death was no less philosophical. If Corman's science fiction pictures mostly explore external threats to individual and communal wellbeing, his Poe pictures, following their source material, turn inward and explore the disintegration of individual minds under great pressure from unresolvable existential angst. As Guy Carrell explains in *Premature Burial* (1962): 'I didn't run away from what was inside that coffin, but from what I knew to be inside me' (0:05:31). Similarly, Roderick Usher, convinced of his evil inheritance, fears even as he looks out for his own and his sister's death. Only their dissolution, he believes, will eradicate the Usher plague.

Fig. 5 *Gas-s-s-s*

By turning from Atomic monsters and global catastrophe to psychological terrors and individual human suffering, Corman gave credence to Vincent Price's maxim that 'Man's inhumanity to man is the ever-present spectre before the artist's eyes' (Price & Price 1981: 175). It is not a coincidence, I believe, that Corman's final picture for AIP, *Gas-s-s-s; or, It Became Necessary to Destroy the World in Order to Save It* (1970), brought together the apocalyptic themes of his science fiction films and the existential angst of his Poe pictures. In the course of the sixties, Corman's 'films and politics' had become 'more radical, more "liberated"' (Corman 1998: 165). The director believed that his films 'should be on the counterculture side' (1998: 166). In making his last AIP picture, Corman completely disregarded his principle to include socio-political criticism and dark psychology only as subtext (Garris 2014). In *House of Usher* evil had been a family affair, and an affair of the mind above all. *Gas-s-s*, for all its whimsy, points the apocalyptic finger straight at Western civilisation's military-industrial complex and its technocratic society. Western materialist ideology becomes a collective madness. Having lost faith in the powers that be, Corman still believed in Poe. He resurrected the Romantic misfit as a spirit-guide for his hippies, riding into the frame on a chopper at significant moments to warn the youthful wanderers of the consequences of their thoughts and actions. Poe tells them that 'flight [from responsibility] may be the most reckless solution' (0:21:41) and points out that even though the young will inherit the world, they too, like their parents, will 'have every opportunity to achieve wickedness' (0:21:51). Fortunately, the hippies heed Poe's warning and fulfil their quest to find and join a utopian community where violence and injustice will be seen 'nevermore' (1:13:32), as the raven on Poe's shoulder croaks at the end of the film. Ironically, the author whose Romantic allegory of a disintegrating mind had propelled Roger Corman from B-movie maverick to art-horror auteur also rang in the end of Corman's tenure as AIP's star director.

CHAPTER 2: THE PLOT OF *USHER*: REBUILDING THE HOUSE OF POE

Andrew Tudor's analysis of 990 horror films produced between 1931 and 1984 reveals that most horror plots follow 'the traditional order-disorder-order sequence' (1989: 19). On top of this, 'the vast majority of films focus upon a specifiable monster rather than on a diffuse threat' (1989: 21) to create the disorder that drives the drama. Tudor's research explains why nineteenth-century horror stories like *Frankenstein* (1818), *Carmilla* (1872), *Jekyll and Hyde* (1886) and *Dracula* (1897) have been adapted so often for the screen. They each contain a clearly identifiable monster whose intrusion into an otherwise realistic fictional universe disrupts the status quo. The eventual defeat or expulsion of the monster restores order, even if the status quo proves irreversibly altered as a consequence of the monster's impact. Tudor's analysis also explains why Poe's tales have fared less well, generally, as literary sources for cinema. His short stories contain minimalistic plots with little dramatic action and lack clearly identifiable monsters. Often enough there is not even a status quo to be disrupted, apart from life being disrupted by death. As was explained in chapter one, Poe's tales were designed to have an immediate aesthetic and emotional impact. Structurally, most of them comprise of lengthy introductions leading to the revelation of a horrific or darkly wonderful tableau.

In Poe's philosophy of composition the emphasis lies firmly on the impact of a story's ending, the final image the reader takes away:

> every plot, worth the name, must be elaborated to its *dénouement* before anything be attempted with the pen. It is only with the *dénouement* constantly in view that we can give a plot its indispensable air of consequence, or causation, by making the incidents, and especially the tone at all points, tend to the development of the intention. (*ER* 1984: 13)

When Poe classified a story's denouement as the most significant aspect of its plot, he used the term not in the traditional sense, denoting a story's resolution, in which conflicts and tensions developed during the rising action of the drama are resolved. Poe often condensed the final three parts of the classic dramatic plot structure – the climax, falling action and denouement – into a single catastrophe in which the protagonist experiences *anagnorisis* (discovery, insight) and *peripeteia* (a change/reversal of fortune) almost simultaneously. This condensation of plot structure leaves no room for a traditional ending that gives the story a sense of closure. But that is the point. The lack of closure is what makes possible the '*elevating excitement of the Soul*'. Poe's best tales in this vein – 'Ligeia', 'Ms. Found in a Bottle', 'The Cask of Amontillado' – all contain careful and balanced 'combinations of event, or tone' (*ER* 1984: 14) and a singular 'climactic effect' (*ER* 1984: 20) that give their plots a vortex-like quality. The ever-increasing suspense pulls the reader further and further into the central dark mystery of the story, where, once arrived, it leaves him or her suspended in a dizzying feeling of wondrous terror.

'The Fall of the House of Usher' (1839) is often classified as the story that epitomises Poe's philosophy of composition. From the outset it hurtles towards a dreadful and inescapable catastrophe from which only the narrator escapes to tell the tale. Adapting Poe properly for the screen means following Poe's method of plotting for unity of effect as well as translating the story's atmosphere of doom, hysterical characterisation, and macabre themes of death and decay into a language understandable to actors, cinematographers and all the various artists involved in the production design. In this chapter, a comparative formal analysis of Richard Matheson's script and Poe's story will show that Matheson indeed followed Poe's philosophy of composition carefully, adapting the nineteenth-century writer's literary conventions to create a cinematic narrative of high fidelity to its literary source that was also very filmable and appealing to the audience of the day. Following the Ushers on their downward spiral towards inevitable dissolution without any sense of escape must have been a novel movie-going experience for an audience used to watching American society saved from alien invaders by intrepid heroes at the drive-in.

THE STRUCTURE OF POE'S 'HOUSE'

The definitive version of 'The Fall of the House of Usher' was published in Whiley and Putnam's *Tales* (1845). It consists of forty-one paragraphs and contains the allegorical poem, 'The Haunted Palace', roughly at the centre of the tale. The exposition in which the setting, protagonist and central theme of the story are introduced takes up the first twelve paragraphs. The next twenty-six paragraphs contain the drawn-out rising action, in which the narrator is confronted with various conundrums surrounding the Usher family's history, and in which the suspense concerning Roderick and Madeline's fate reaches a fever pitch. The catastrophe in which Roderick reveals his secret, Madeline reappears and confronts her brother and the house sinks into the tarn, comprises just three paragraphs of roughly equal length that together should generate the '*elevating excitement of the soul*' in the reader.

To achieve the desired intensity of terror and wonder at the catastrophe, Poe creates a mood of deep, soporific melancholy at the outset of the tale:

> During the whole of a dull, dark, and soundless day in the autumn of the year, when clouds hung oppressively low in the heavens, I had been passing alone, on horseback, through a singularly dreary track of country; and at length found myself, as the shades of the evening drew on, within view of the melancholy House of Usher. (2000: 397)

Not only the bleak imagery, but the use of alveolar alliteration and sonorous vowels throughout this opening sentence invoke and sustain the 'sense of insufferable gloom' (ibid.) that overcomes the narrator. A key detail in the narrator's description of the environment that guides the reader's understanding of the image is his explanation that 'there was an iciness, a sinking, a sickening of the heart – an unredeemed dreariness of thought which no goading of the imagination could torture into aught of the sublime' (ibid.). This remarkably down-beat tone foregrounds the low-ebb of the narrator's thoughts, and the Ushers' well-being, which will greatly contrast with the kinetic, harrowing catastrophe, at which the 'mystery all insoluble' (ibid.) threatens, but ultimately fails to completely reveal itself to the reader.

The second and third paragraphs comprise the backstory concerning the Usher family, Roderick's relation to the narrator – they are boyhood friends – and his 'acute bodily illness' and 'mental disorder' (2000: 398). The narrator highlights the family's 'deeds of munificent yet unobtrusive charity' as well as their peculiar artistic temperament and explains that 'the entirely family lay in the direct line of descent' (2000: 399). Apart from setting the mood and introducing the protagonist, these opening paragraphs introduce the central motif of the story: the house and its inhabitants have become one and are slowly decaying in their symbiosis. An observant reader will notice the personification of the house in the opening paragraph: it is described as melancholy with 'vacant eye-like windows' (a phrase repeated in the closing words of the first paragraph). This personification is enhanced by the narrator's explanation that, in the minds of 'the peasantry' living in the surrounding area, the name Usher denoted 'both the family and the family mansion' (ibid.). Clearly, this story asks to be read as an allegory: the house resembles a mind falling into decay, as Richard Wilbur (1966) has noted.

As a materialisation of Roderick's mind, the house is as much the protagonist of the tale as its master. It is described first and in great detail, characterised by an 'excessive antiquity', overspread with 'Minute fungi', showing 'a wild inconsistency between its still perfect adaptation of parts, and the crumbling condition of the individual stones', with 'a barely perceptible fissure' running across the façade from top to bottom and 'a pestilent and mystic vapor, dull, sluggish, faintly discernible, and leaden-hued' (2000: 400) enveloping all. Yet the narrator is quick to stifle the reader's sense of wonder by rejecting any thought of supernatural agency as 'a strange fancy' (2000: 399), the product of a temporarily over-active imagination. By rejecting his fancies, the narrator seeks to control the reader's response, but the discerning reader will not miss the parallel established by Poe between the house and Roderick, with his skin of 'ghastly pallor', eyes of 'miraculous lustre', straggly 'silken hair' of a 'wild gossamer texture' (2000: 402). It is the potential discrepancy between the narrator's and reader's interpretation of events that generates the suspense and eventual wonder.

Roderick spends his days in a 'large and lofty' room with a 'black oaken floor' and high windows through which 'feeble gleams of encrimsoned light made their way through trellised pains'. It is filled with 'comfortless, antique, and tattered' furniture, and littered with 'books and musical instruments'. The farthest corners remain forever in shadow and on entering the narrator believed he 'breathed an atmosphere of sorrow' (2000: 401). Just as Roderick's countenance mirrors the house, the interior of the house reflects Roderick's spirit. While the narrator again fails to openly acknowledge the parallel, the reader is free to establish the link. For the reader who takes the allegorical approach, Poe's story is about psychological, rather than supernatural, demons. Roderick describes his illness as 'a constitutional and a family evil' (2000: 402). He fears what he already knows is inevitable: the decay of his body and his mind: 'I must perish in this deplorable folly. Thus, thus, and not otherwise, shall I be lost' (2000: 403). Poe cleverly puns on the word 'folly' here combining its general meaning, a sense of 'foolishness', with its specific architectural meaning: 'Follies are fashionable or frantic, built to keep up with the neighbours, or built from obsession. They are cheerful and morbid, both an ornament for a gentleman's grounds and a mirror for his mind' (Jones 1974: 1). The narrator does not recognise this pun.

The exposition ends with Roderick's description of his illness: the 'morbid acuteness of the senses' (2000: 403) that has left him living in the shadows, eating only 'the most insipid food' and enjoying only the sound of his own peculiar compositions. Roderick confides to his friend that 'the period will sooner or later arrive when I must abandon life and reason altogether, in some struggle with the grim phantasm, FEAR' (ibid.). The personification of fear foregrounds the allegorical nature of the tale. It foreshadows the catastrophe in which Roderick's sister Madeline – his only kin – rises from her untimely entombment to unite with her brother in a deathly embrace. Roderick knows his own family will be his undoing.

Roderick's confession marks a turning point in the narrative. It sets in motion the narrator's first critical reflections on what exactly holds Roderick in the grip of fear. The initial question that the narrator faces during the rising action is an epistemological one. Will he be able to explain matters through empirical observation and analysis of the facts, or should he accept Roderick's intuitive knowledge that the family and the house have come to share a single soul and together breathe the putrid atmosphere of the rotten environment, which they have cultivated themselves? Further complications arise for the narrator when Roderick wavers between natural and supernatural explanations of his plight. In the first paragraph of the rising action he puts his fear down to the influence of the mansion's peculiar fabric on his physical and mental wellbeing. In the next paragraph he attributes his mental and physical sufferings to anxieties over his sister Madeline's mysterious illness – 'a gradual wasting away of the person' (2000: 404) that has stumped the family physician. This juxtaposition of natural and supernatural explanations and the narrator's determination to give credence to the former and dispel the latter further heightens suspense. The reader can interpret Madeline as a symbolic figure, representing what Roderick knows intuitively but fears to acknowledge.

Refusing to believe Roderick, and judging his host of unsettled mind, the narrator is determined to alleviate his friend's sorrows by means of distraction. Consequently, the following paragraphs detail an interlude in which the narrator and Roderick actively seek relief from tension by engaging in various creative pursuits. While this interlude represents a lull in the tensions between narrator and protagonist, it further heightens the mystery in the mind of the reader. Roderick's artistic productions are abstract: 'if ever mortal painted an idea, that mortal was Roderick Usher' (ibid.). To express an abstract idea in figurative terms is to construct a symbol, or an allegory. The symbolic meaning of Roderick's painting remains obtuse to the narrator. It is 'an immensely long and rectangular vault or tunnel with low walls, smooth, white, and without interruption or device', apparently lying 'at an exceeding depth below the surface of the earth' yet lit by 'intense rays' that 'bathed the whole in a ghastly and inappropriate splendour' (2000: 406). Just as Roderick's dark drawing room is a reflection of his mind, his painting is an abstract rendering of 'the soul imprisoned in the coffins of the body, of the house, and of the cosmos itself' (Heller 1987: 132).

The allegorical ballad that Roderick sings in the next paragraph functions as a key to the story, despite the narrator's dismissal of its import. 'The Haunted Palace' had been published as a stand-alone poem in the April 1839 issue of the *American Museum of Science, Literature and the Arts*. The story of 'Usher' can be considered a prose elaboration of Poe's poem, detailing the 'sense of the inevitability of the spirit's madness within its bodily prison, the unavoidable surrender of the individual self to disintegration' (ibid.). In the poem, the 'fair and stately palace' is a human head in which 'the monarch Thought' resides. Initially, the music coming out of the palace door is a tribute to 'The wit and wisdom of their king'. But the grand hall is invaded by 'evils things, in robes of sorrow', leaving visitors peering through 'the red-litten windows' at 'Vast forms that move fantastically / To a discordant melody' (2000: 406-408); the king has gone mad.

For a reader who recognises the poem as an allegorical representation of the central theme of the story, the ballad is a revelation. Here is the first moment of true excitement of the soul. Crucially, at this moment the interpretive path of the ideal reader and the narrator diverge. The narrator remarks that 'in the under or mystic current of its meaning, I fancied that I perceived, and for the first time, a full consciousness on the part of Usher, of the tottering of his lofty reason upon her throne' (2000: 406). While the narrator rationalises the 'mystic current' of the ballad as a product of Roderick's fancy, the reader of the tale is able to interpret 'The Haunted Palace' as a key to Poe's allegory on the insignificance of the human soul in the cosmic scheme of things. The narrator explains that the performance of the ballad led to a discussion of 'the sentience of all vegetable things' (2000: 408), even 'the gray stones of the home of his forefathers' (ibid.). On this theory of the unity of house and inhabitants the narrator concludes: 'Such opinions need no comment, and I will make none' (2000: 406). He does not believe in Usher's vision and calls him 'a hypochondriac' (2000: 409). The narrator's pejorative statements invite the reader to judge the situation for him- or herself. Poe is asking the reader: what do you see? Do you agree with the narrator's interpretation of events or do you believe Roderick's explanation?

I believe Roderick is right. Poe's use of personification, metaphor, symbol and allegory, gives the reader many hints that the narrative's central theme is spiritual, rather than material. It is about Roderick's struggle to face death and his fear of the unknown that awaits him in the afterlife, if there is an afterlife. The paragraph listing Roderick's books underscores his obsession with the existence (or non-existence) of a spirit world. Poe would not have expected his readers to be familiar with the most obscure esoteric volumes in Usher's library. He would have expected them to recognise the popular names of Fludd, Campanella, and especially Emanuel Swedenborg, 'the most influential European esotericist for nineteenth-century America' (Versluis 2001: 17). The titles in his library, like Swedenborg's popular *Heaven and Hell*, characterise Roderick as a spiritual quester. The discovery that he has made, about his ancestors' past and his own future, is not heavenly, however, but hellish. After all, the vault in which Madeline is buried was used 'in remote feudal times, for the worst purposes of a donjon-keep, and, in later days, as a place of deposit for powder, or some other highly combustible substance' (2000: 410). The Ushers, who 'of late' are known for 'repeated deeds of munificent yet unobtrusive charity' (2000: 399), have a violent past. They are like Nathaniel Hawthorne's Pyncheon family, hiding a heritage of cruelty and injustice behind a stately facade. What Usher fears is that he will find himself in Hell after death. Roderick would have learned from Swedenborg that there is such a thing as 'inherited evil' (Swedenborg 1995: 455) and that man makes his own heaven or hell, depending on his thoughts and actions while alive (Swedenborg 1995: 446). A reader who recognises the allegorical nature of the story will be able to empathise with Roderick, who believes he has inherited and cannot escape his family's past; a reader who seeks for a rational explanation, like the narrator, will be baffled by the catastrophe.

In Poe's tale, the catastrophe is heralded when Roderick reveals that he and his friend had entombed Madeline alive. According to the narrator, Roderick's confession of this act – the inescapable effect of his evil inheritance – was spoken 'in a low, hurried, and gibbering murmur, as if [he was] unconscious of [his friend's] presence' (2000: 416). During this and the final two paragraphs the narrator is merely an observer of, and not a participant in, the action. Roderick, immersed in his thoughts, seems to be speaking to himself and not to the narrator. His ghastly confession is a soliloquy, not a monologue. So when Roderick eventually shrieks: '*Madman!* I tell you that she now stands without the door!' (ibid.), he must be addressing himself. The 'She' is of course Madeline, but Madeline is a symbolic figure in the tale, appearing only twice, once in the shadows of Roderick's chamber (his mind) and now when Roderick finally acknowledges his fate. Madeline represents what Roderick always knew but could not acknowledge: his own death by the hand of his inheritance. When 'Madeline [falls] heavily inward upon the person of her brother, and in her violent and now final death-agonies, [bears] him to the floor a corpse, and a victim to the terrors he had anticipated' (2000: 416-7) the allegory of 'The Haunted Palace' is completed: Roderick has gone insane, finally, and has fallen into the hell he has constructed for himself during his lifetime.

'MAD HOUSE': MATHESON'S NEW BUILD ON POE'S FOUNDATIONS

In an interview with Tim Lucas, Roger Corman explains that he was familiar with Richard Matheson's *I am Legend* (1954), *The Shrinking Man* (1956) and several of his short stories. Even though Matheson personally did not care much for Poe, Corman believed him to be the perfect writer to adapt Poe for the silver screen. Matheson's writing belongs to the post-war gothic renaissance inaugurated by Fritz Leiber's *Conjure Wife* (1943) and most famously embodied by Shirley Jackson's *The Haunting of Hill House* (1959). Much post-war gothic fiction explored the dark psychological and social forces at play behind the white picket-fenced idyll of the middle-class American household. Matheson's 'Mad House' (1954) shows that he was just as adept at constructing allegories of disintegrating human minds as Poe.

Chris Neal is the master of Matheson's 'Mad House'. He is a forty-year old lecturer in English, and aspiring writer, who is frustrated with the turn his life has taken since he married his college sweetheart Sally. Matheson's tale opens with descriptions of outlandishly angry outbursts by Chris in response to everyday domestic mishaps: a broken pencil tip, a malfunctioning typewriter, a blunt razor, a broken thread of dental floss. While Chris remains unaware, the reader is privy to 'a rustle in the wastebasket' (2002: 68) into which the pencil was thrown, and witnesses 'the cover of the machine slip down' as 'the keys trembled in their slots' (2002: 69). The narrator describes how Chris's violent outbursts are actually infecting his house: 'Sprays of teeth grinding hysteria clouding his windows and falling to his floors. Oceans of wild, uncontrolled hate flooding through every room of his house; filling each iota of space with a shifting, throbbing life' (2002: 71). Suffering from 'the sickness of despair, of lost ambition' (ibid.), Chris feels 'a vague sense of forestalling doom' (2002: 79). Unable, or unwilling to locate the origin of his despair in himself, Chris believes that 'some revenging power had taken roost in the house, pouring a savage life into inanimate things. Threatening him' (2002: 80).

Like Poe's 'Usher', Matheson's 'Mad House' contains a spiritual theme at heart. In a moment of reflection Chris becomes aware of a fault line in the dominant ideology. A man either 'devoted his life to his work or to his wife and children and home. It could not be combined; not in this day and age. In this insane world where God was second to income and goodness to wealth' (2002: 86). Chris's despair turns out to be an existential crisis. He realises that in the pursuit of social status (a full professorship at Fort College) and material comfort, he has neglected the welfare of his soul, and comes to the conclusion that 'I would rather have my soul intact than the suit of clothes I wear' (ibid.). The discrepancy between what he feels is his true self and the role he currently plays in society has become so large that he now feels entirely 'apart from the city, the country, the world' (2002: 87). This alienation has left him feeling like 'a ghost' (ibid.).

The fantastic aspect of the tale is introduced in the shape of Chris's best friend, Dr Morton, a psychologist with academic interests in paranormal phenomena. The absence of a first name for Dr Morton is indicative of Chris's alienation. He can only approach his friend in his professional capacity as a (more successful) colleague. It turns out that Morton has been keeping a close eye on Chris and his house. During their brief encounter in the story, Morton tries to persuade Chris that his negative energy is feeding into the house's structure: 'it goes into your rooms, and into your furniture and into the air. It goes into Sally. It makes everything sick; including you. It crowds you out. It welds a link between animate and inanimate. *Psychobolie*....You're poisoning your house' (2002: 91). Chris's tragic flaw that results in his death is his failure to believe in his friend and colleague's paranormal explanation of events: 'It's just an empty house, he thought ... nothing but a house' (2002: 98). Chris's inability to act on the insight he gains concerning the source of his suffering – his disappointment with and alienation from mainstream culture – has made him a victim of this culture. His suburban home – the iconic symbol of this culture – is literally consuming his identity: 'What was it? This feeling that he was sinking into the couch, into the floorboards, dissolving in the air, joining the molecules of the house' (2002: 100). Just as Roderick Usher was afraid to confront his fears of death and the afterlife, Chris 'refused to accept the instinctive fear in himself', says that 'it might only be in the mind', and concludes: 'it had to be imagination' (2002: 100-101).

Matheson's 'Mad House' reveals that the author's interest in the haunted house formula lay in its potential to function as a vehicle for the exploration of psychological and spiritual, rather than material or historical themes. Corman believed that 'the world of Poe, to a large extent, was the world of the unconscious' (qtd in Naha 1982: 31). His understanding of Matheson as writer of similarly psychological horror, may well have made him conclude that he was 'the ideal writer to adapt Poe to the screen' (French 2007: 13). Poe's tale, because of its allegorical nature and complex psychological themes, gave Matheson exactly the kind of old materials from which he could build something new. Being 'close to Poe', for Matheson and Corman meant producing a portrait of an isolated and fearful man's descent into madness and ultimately death.

THE *HOUSE OF USHER* SCRIPT

One of the difficulties Matheson encountered when he set out to adapt 'The Fall of the House of Usher' for the movies was that 'the story was so simple ... you had a few people stuck in an old house' (qtd in Naha 1982: 30). The success of William Castle's

House on Haunted Hill (1959) had proven that films *about* people stuck in an old house could scare 'the pants off every child in America' (Price 1999: 177). But Robb White's script was full of dramatic action and shock effects. In White's old house something was happening every scene and skeletons flew over the audience. In Poe's house all was dreary and still as the grave, and with an AIP budget to work with, Matheson must have realised that Corman was unlikely to approve a treatment that asked him to outdo Castle's 'Emergo' effect. AIP's dubious track record when it came to special effects (remember *It Conquered the World?*) may also have influenced Matheson's decision to 'not ... write *The House of Usher* as a 'monster' movie' (qtd in Naha 1982: 30). Instead, he 'tried to get it as close to Poe's original as possible', adding only 'a romance to the story' (French 2007: 370) and a handful of original scenes to enhance continuity. Also the character of the Ushers' servant – named Bristol in the film – was fleshed out to assist exposition and clarify character motivation.

Rather than hindering Matheson, Poe's original story and AIP's limited budget played to his strengths as a writer of psychological horror. Corman accepted the first draft of Matheson's script. Vincent Price was equally impressed. The actor believed 'the works of Edgar Allan Poe hadn't been done properly on the screen', and was pleased to find that 'what Roger tried to do was to express some of the psychology of Poe's characters'. In doing this correctly, Price believed Matheson had grasped 'the essence of Poe' (Price 1999: 211).

Matheson's exposition runs nearly parallel to Poe's. He imagines an opening scene in which a man called Philip Winthrop – the film's embodiment of Poe's nameless narrator – rides through 'a bleak and lifeless' region resembling 'some Doré-esque nether region' or 'some dolorous moonscape' (French 2007: 55). Matheson's imagination perfectly translates into visual imagery the gloom-laden mood established by Poe's opening paragraph. Instead of inserting a flashback that details the backstory about the narrator's friendship with Roderick and the Usher family history (paragraph 2 and 3 in Poe's tale), Matheson's script suggests that the viewer should be immediately confronted with (a matte painting of) 'the infamous structure' (French 2007: 56). Poe created mystery by minutely detailing the narrator's ambiguous emotional responses to the surroundings. Matheson creates mystery by carefully pacing the way in which these surroundings are presented to the audience. Taking Philip's point of view, 'the CAMERA EXAMINES the house' (French 2007: 56), revealing all the same structural and aesthetic peculiarities noticed by the narrator in Poe's tale: a mansion of great antiquity with discoloured but intact stones covered with 'a webbing of minute fungi … like some hideous moldering lace' that give the impression that the 'decay is *inner*: that every separate stone is honey-combed with rot' (ibid.), and 'a narrow zigzag fissure running from the roof to the black waters of the tarn' (French 2007: 57). Close-ups of the matte painting (discussed in detail in chapter 3) translate Matheson's word paintings into striking visuals.

As in Poe's tale, the first dramatic scene is the servant's reception of the visitor. Here Matheson inserts the first original scene in which Philip tells Bristol: 'Miss Usher and I are engaged to be married' (French 2007: 58). This statement introduces the audience to Matheson's dramatic addition to Poe's story: Roderick, the brother, and Philip, the lover, will vie for the possession of Madeline, the ill-fated gothic heroine. Poe purists may cringe at this change in characterisation. By turning Roderick's baffled friend into his antagonist, Poe's story comes closer to a traditional gothic melodrama like Universal's *Black Castle* (1952). But in Matheson's script – unlike Universal's gothic potboiler – the romance angle is a red herring. It allows Matheson to give the audience an initial sense of traditional order – the Usher line of descent – being challenged by the intrusion of an outsider: the lover Philip Winthrop. Bristol's nervous rejection of Philip – 'I cannot admit you, sir' (ibid.) – and Philip's challenge to his authority – 'Cannot? By whose order?' (ibid.) – signal to the audience that a classic gothic conflict of interests concerning marriage, lineage and property will ensue. But as the intrusive outsider forcing entry into a home, Philip occupies the position of the monster, on a structural level, which is one of Matheson's clever twists to the traditional horror plot. Poe's original source material gave Matheson an ancient family with a dubious legacy, a hysterical protagonist, and a befuddled narrator. There really is no antagonist in Poe's tale, only characters who are their own worst enemy. To Matheson's credit, he managed to hold on to this ambiguity. At first, Philip seems to be a brash youth, who challenges the patriarchal authority of the master of the house. Teenage audiences can identify with his tenacious attitude towards the older white-haired brother of his beloved. The first quarter of the picture suggests that this is a film of generational conflict. By the end, however, the roles of protagonist and antagonist have reversed. Philip 'fails to understand the forces at work within the house' (Jancovich 1996: 279) and turns out to be as befuddled as Poe's narrator about what is going on, and impotent to put his valiant rescue plans into action. Roderick turns out to have been right about his own and Madeline's fate.

Matheson marks Roderick as the true protagonist of the story in the same way that Poe does: by closely detailing in parallel the interior of the mansion and the features of its master. Poe uses evocative diction to create parallels between the look of the house and Roderick's features. Matheson constructs parallel scenes to create a similar allegorical effect. At first, Philip is seen journeying through the barren landscape, up to the front door of the house, which suddenly opens to reveal a mystified servant; next, he journeys through a gloomy gothic interior cluttered with 'huge, antique and worn' furniture and 'armorial trophies' with 'deep-hued drapes and tapestries' (French 2007: 62) hanging on the walls, only to be surprised again by a suddenly opening door. This time it is Roderick who appears, exclaiming in an irritated tone: 'what is the meaning of this?' (2007: 63). Bristol has guided Philip to Roderick, Roderick in turn will guide Philip into the innermost chambers of his mind.

By the end of the exposition, Poe ensures that his reader becomes curious about Roderick's character by leaving his narrator wondering exactly what has caused his friend Roderick to be caught in the grip of 'FEAR', and a state of extreme nervous agitation. Matheson similarly draws the viewer to Roderick's point of view at the end of the exposition, by characterising Philip as a well-meaning, but single-minded and stubborn young man. He has only one aim, to take Madeline away from the House of Usher, and remains unconvinced by, or uninterested in, Roderick's explanations of the family curse. By contrast, Roderick is presented as a suffering soul, conscious of the peculiarity of his explanations, but convinced through experience of their truth. While Roderick explains that 'the Usher line is tainted!' (French 2007: 70) and that he and Madeline are 'two pale drops of fire guttering in the vast consuming darkness' (2007: 73), Philip believes Roderick is exaggerating and plays down his fears: 'perhaps your family does have (he searches for the diplomatic phrase) certain peculiarities of temperament' (2007: 72). The stage directions guiding Mark Damon's delivery suggest that Philip is not supposed to invoke sympathy: 'trying to be pleasant', 'stiffening', 'coolly', 'shocked', 'defensively', 'trying to understand', 'tensely', 'incredulous' (2007: 69-71). He is merely impatient to take his bride-to-be back to Boston and seems not to care about Roderick's welfare at all. In contrast to Price's poetic diction and musical tones, Damon is either stern and emotionless, or bursting out in anger.

In a complete reversal of the traditional Gothic plot – in which the lustful and power-hungry patriarch is confronted by a valiant hero of superior morality – Matheson exposes a conflict between an older sensitive neurotic and a youthful, headstrong, but foolish lover. Therefore, the love-plot, while an addition to Poe's original, does little damage to the essence of Poe's tale, which is to evoke 'an elevating excitement of the Soul' (ER 1984: 93) through the contemplation of the terrible sense of wonder Roderick experiences in confronting his own fears of the dark fate he knows he and his sister cannot escape.

The rising action commences with a second original scene that develops the antagonism between Philip and Roderick. Having felt the house move and noticing the fissure in the wall, Philip is on the way down to dinner when he can only just save himself from a 'huge urn' (French 2007: 77) falling on top of him (a chandelier in the finished film). The rising action in Poe's story commences with the narrator detailing Roderick's belief that the life of the house and the lives of its occupants are supernaturally linked. This brief additional action sequence has the same function as the first paragraph of the rising action in Poe's tale. It visually draws a parallel between Roderick's earlier request: 'will you go?' and Philip's reply, 'I will not' (2007: 74). Like Roderick in the earlier scene, the house has begun to moan, and Philip's narrow escape suggests that it shares Roderick's desire for him to leave.

Roderick and Philip discuss the dilapidated state of the mansion and the barren grounds during the original dinner scene. As in the earlier dialogue, Philip is unsympathetically characterised through his insistence on rational explanations: '"his logical" mind is incapable of comprehending either Roderick's or Madeline's situation or the meanings of their actions' (Jancovich 1996: 279). The rationalist non-believer is often an early victim in supernatural horror tales. By contrast, Roderick's character takes on an increased sense of mystery when Madeline stops him from apparently revealing something about the family history and grounds that will truly shock Philip: 'please, brother' (French 2007: 81). Usher's unspoken explanation concerning the barren soil of the grounds leaves the viewer in a state of suspense concerning the mysterious goings on. For the curious viewer, Philip's disinterest in any of Roderick's explanations make him an obstacle rather than a guide toward discovering the terrible truth of the Usher heritage. If Philip has his way, the audience will never know what truly haunts Roderick and Madeline.

Poe's story and Matheson's script converge after dinner. In Poe's tale, tension is heightened by introducing the peculiar artistic temperament of the Ushers, and Roderick specifically: 'if ever mortal painted an idea' (Poe 2000: 405). These paragraphs serve to introduce the allegorical features of the story. In Poe's story, Roderick's abstract painting and his ballad 'The Haunted Palace' are works of art through which Roderick gives shape to his forebodings of doom. In Matheson's script, the paintings in Roderick's drawing room (discussed in more detail in chapter 3) are visible to the audience and speak for themselves, so Philip does not have to comment on them directly. Similarly, the audience can listen with Philip to the 'eerie fantasia' (French 2007: 82) Roderick plays on his lute, while the camera closes in to reveal 'his sensitive, pain-wracked features' (2007: 83). Just as in Poe's story the narrator fails to fully recognise the prophetic import of Roderick's art, Philip responds to the art only with stock phrases like 'remarkable', while the audience can draw their own conclusion about the picture of the flaming house and spectral portrait of Madeline. Philip's conventional response to Roderick's unconventional artworks reveals that he is out of touch with the Ushers' experience of the world. His commandeering claim, 'If I do leave, I won't be alone, I –' (2007: 85) is cut short by a silent Roderick, who turns his back on the protesting youth and walks away. Roderick is finished making requests because Philip refuses to understand. Philip is now on his own in the House, and at the mercy of its will.

Further complications ensue in the original scenes that follow. Having failed to persuade Roderick to let Madeline go, and unable to rest, Philip seeks out his beloved's room to persuade her to 'leave this house tomorrow' (French 2007: 87). To his dismay he finds Madeline willing, but hesitant, to leave: 'If only I could … may you never see into the heart of this terrible house' (ibid.). Rather than trying to understand his fiancé, Philip 'continually bullies and invalidates Madeline' (Jancovich 1996: 279). As will be discussed in more detail in chapter 4, Madeline is a highly unusual gothic heroine. She combines a strong, independent personality with a conviction of the Usher curse. By being simultaneously understanding of Philip's perspective, yet convinced of her family's fate, she resembles Roderick to a large extent. Madeline tells Philip a story of her family that dovetails with Roderick's later history (in which paragraph 12 and 19 of Poe story are incorporated). This further alienates Philip from the Ushers. And it starts to look like he will fail in his lover's quest.

In order to allow AIP's target audience to understand the development of the plot, Matheson included a concrete evil that the audience expected to be revealed at some point during the picture, and which allowed them to understand the human characters' motivations and actions. This is how genre pictures work, after all. But the evil that Matheson conjured up was already, if implicitly, present in the original story. Poe's narrator explains that the Usher vault had been a dungeon in the past and vaguely sketches a violent history for the Ushers. Matheson expands on this hint by creating a 'plague of evil' (French 2007: 118) passed down from one Usher to the next. Not a single audience member can fail to acknowledge the pernicious influence of this heritage on the suffering Roderick and Madeline.

The audience will learn that Roderick and Madeline were born into evil, in the sense of having been born into a family defined by their crimes. One of their ancestors had been a 'Swindler. Forger. Jewel thief. Drug addict'; another a 'professional assassin'; another a 'Blackmailer. Harlot. *Murderess*'; yet another a 'Smuggler. Slave trader. Mass Murderer' (French 2007: 119-20). Usher is convinced that his family's evil ways are a disease: 'it flows in our veins, Mr. Winthrop … it is our inheritance' (2007: 122). By locking himself and his sister in the ancestral home, Matheson's Roderick is trying to stop the spread of evil by killing off the final two branches of the family tree before they flower. Suddenly, the atmospheric opening scene containing the blackened lifeless trees takes on a symbolic meaning. The end of life on the Usher estate will also mean the end of the Ushers' evil reign. 'Evil is not just a word, Mr Winthrop. It is a reality … *the house, itself, is evil now*', Roderick explains, and as long as the Ushers' prolong the family line, the evil will spread. The film's monster is a concept: the stifling influence of psychological, material and even legal inheritance.

Just as the reader of Poe's story is drawn into the mind of Usher, the rising action of Matheson's script steers the audience's sympathy towards the sensitive and suffering Roderick, rather than the recalcitrant Philip who, like Matheson's Chris Neal, does 'not believe in the sins of the fathers being visited upon the children', and remains adamant that the House of Usher 'is only a house' (French 2007: 120) and that Roderick's words are 'sickened fancies' (2007: 123). In Matheson's script – as in the finished film – Roderick is left standing 'trembling with pain and anguished fury' (ibid.). The audience becomes aware of the inevitability of the approaching catastrophe: if Roderick is right, both he and Madeline are doomed; if Philip wins and takes Madeline away, the Usher evil will spread anew. Imagine the sequel: *Usher II: Madeline's Baby!* Either way, doom will come to Roderick and Madeline. Naturally, the tension increases as any chance of a happy ending eludes the characters: 'There can be no peace without penalty … our blight must be removed from this Earth' (2007: 133).

At this point in Matheson's script Madeline is 'killed off', so to speak. During a heated argument with Roderick, in which the audience hears only Madeline's words, she says: *'I will be free!'* (French 2007: 127), which turns into the more direct 'I will leave' in the finished film. Exactly what she will free herself from, or what she will leave behind, remains ambiguous. Will the Usher curse be lifted when she leaves the house? Or does leaving the house mean being free of Roderick's controlling nature? As the climax draws near, the audience is invited to imagine what exactly Roderick has been saying to Madeline, and to judge the import of Madeline's final words for themselves. When Philip enters her room, Madeline lies lifeless on her bed. Philip accuses Roderick of murder, but Roderick is adamant that it is the Usher illness that has finally overtaken her spirit. Who to believe?

During the burial scene that follows, the audience is shown, and Roderick realises, that Madeline is not yet dead. This creates a significant moment of dramatic irony in the film. From here on Philip is the only character ignorant of her fate. This scene helps to sustain the audience's interest in the plot. They can begin to speculate that Madeline will return, most likely; but how? Will she be alive or a spectre? This scene sets up intimations of the kind of gruesome reveal that has drawn audiences to horror pictures from the outset. Importantly, this dramatic irony puts the audience in the same position as Roderick. With him, the audience has only to wait and pay close attention to any signs of Madeline's resurrection. For the unwitting Philip, Madeline's return from the dead will be a much greater shock.

Poe brings his story to the catastrophe by means of the 'Mad Trist' episode in which the noises within the romance read by the narrator parallel the noises that Roderick hears coming from the crypt. Matheson rightly judged that this static and largely symbolic scene in the story could not be successfully adapted into suspenseful cinema. The audience would never believe that Philip, having stubbornly opposed Roderick throughout the film and accused him of murder, would suddenly wish to sooth Roderick's shattered nerves by reading him a story. The questing hero of Poe's 'Mad Trist' is present in the film though. It is Philip. Learning of Madeline's cataleptic fits, he rushes to save his beloved from premature burial only to find that she has mysteriously vanished from her coffin. Substituting Poe's 'Mad Trist' for Philip's mad dash around the house is another of Matheson's dramatic master strokes. It solves the problem of the passivity of Poe's narrator, and quickens the pace of the narrative as it moves toward a harrowing, kinetic climax.

Matheson's plot challenges conventional notions of heroism, however, as Philip and Roderick exchange positions during the rising action and catastrophe. At the outset of the film, as Hendershot explains, 'Philip is the center of normality and identification' (2000: 223). He is the young lover seeking the hand of his beloved in marriage. Roderick's character is obviously unconventional: the reclusive visionary artist caught in the grip of a family curse. But as Philip's confidence in overcoming Roderick's refusal wanes, his frustration rises, and so does his temper. In contrast to traditional Gothic character arcs, it is not the deranged lord of the manor but the heroine's lover, and the potential hero of the tale, who becomes hysterical and turns to violence, alienating him from the audience's sympathy. Having taken up an axe to destroy the lock on Madeline's casket, and finding it empty, Philip confronts Roderick with the same axe, now raised in a poise to kill. Roderick, obviously disturbed by the unfolding of events, merely retorts: 'Go on. You would be doing me a very great favour' (French 2007: 149). Philip still refuses to believe that Roderick's aim was to end the Usher curse; that the only way this could be done was by sacrificing Madeline and himself. By scarifying himself for a greater cause, no matter how peculiar, Roderick plays the part of a Romantic hero; Philip's increasingly violent demeanour makes him look increasingly like a foil to Roderick. Dropping the axe, Philip 'grabs Roderick by the shoulders roughly. Roderick gasps in pain' and yells '(in agony) don't touch me!' (ibid.). But Philip continues to manhandle Roderick, who is now 'deranged by pain and grief' (2007: 150). Frustrated, and in 'a rush of maniacal fury, Philip clutches at Roderick's throat' (ibid.). This scene foreshadows the catastrophe in which

Fig. 6 The violent hero

Madeline will actually achieve what Philip fails to do. Philip's increasing verbal and physical aggression towards the pitiful Roderick places Roderick firmly in the position of victim rather than villain. Yet, as a quester, seeking to save his beloved, Philip, for all his violence, cannot be cast in the role of villain, creating the moral ambiguity that characterises Poe's tale. It turns out that really there is no battle between good and evil here, just two opposing perspectives of an insoluble mystery about the Usher family.

The rising action quickly reaches a fever pitch as 'Philip trashes around wildly' (French 2007: 153) in the cellar and, 'completely exhausted' (ibid.) is brought back to his room by Bristol. The original dream sequence which follows is a transitional scene preparing the way for the catastrophe. The way in which the dream is scripted by Matheson and directed by Corman reveals the influence of Freudian psychology, which was a popular approach to the workings of the unconscious in the 1950s. Corman has often spoken and written about his interest in Freudian theory and his Freudian take on Poe (see Corman 1998: 77-81). As a student of Freud, Corman would have found out that, according to Freud, 'dreams are the language of the unconscious: and since ... the unconscious consists entirely of sexual wishes, dreams relate to such repressed wishes' (Hadfield 1970: 18). In the dream sequence, Philip descends into the Usher chapel only to be beleaguered by the ghosts of all Ushers past. As 'he struggles in their midst ... Roderick is carrying the unconscious Madeline through a doorway' (French 2007: 156). The lack of any disorientating displacement or condensation in the dream sequence, allows the teenage audience to gain unfiltered access to Philip's (sexual) desires, which are very straightforward: he wants Madeline, but her ancestors, and the last living heir to the estate are blocking his way to success.

When Philip awakens from his dream, the storm has risen, signalling to any experienced horror-movie goer that the climax is at hand. An un-filmed shot scripted by Matheson reveals the extent to which intimations of the supernatural were part of the overall atmosphere of the film. As Philip looks out into the 'agitated darkness' (French 2007: 158), he notices that 'everything in sight glows with the unearthly light of some luminous gas which hangs above the land' (ibid.). It is a pity that this shot was never included in the picture. It is the kind of visual effect the Corman crew were adept at producing, and it would have further enhanced the eerie atmosphere, giving more credence to Roderick's perspective of events.

In Poe's original, it is Roderick who first realises that the catastrophe is at hand. It is he who searches out the narrator as the storm rises. In the script, Matheson's misguided quester searches out the depressed Roderick when he hears the sounds of his guitar over the howling storm wind. Entering the room, Philip looks down on Roderick's 'pain-rigid face' with 'maleficent eyes' (French 2007: 159). Oblivious to the portentous nature of the storm, Philip makes himself look quite silly by threatening to bring Roderick to justice for the murder of his sister. Roderick's calm and 'sardonically' toned responses to Philip's 'venomously' (ibid.) delivered threats further enhance the viewer's sympathy for the doomed protagonist. The audience knows with Roderick that Madeline will return to seal the siblings' doom.

In adapting Poe's catastrophe for the cinema, Matheson was faced with one crucial formal problem. Poe, working in the medium of prose fiction, could shift the narrator's role from one paragraph to the next: historian, participant, observer, analyst. Matheson, working in the medium of film, could allow Philip no such freedom. Speaking aloud to himself while wandering the corridors at night would make Philip look ridiculous, adding an unwanted comedic touch to the film. Adding a voice-over would interrupt the claustrophobic atmosphere created by the *mise-en-scène* and would slow down the pace of a film with already very little dramatic action. In order to express his thoughts, Philip has to be in situations in which he can engage in heated conversation with Bristol, Madeline or Roderick. Still, Matheson followed Poe by foregrounding the role of Roderick during the catastrophe and marginalising Philip's presence during the final dialogues. Just as in the story, the catastrophe commences with Roderick's confession of having heard various noises from below: 'I heard every sound she made ... her – *breathing* in the casket ... *the scratching of her nails upon the lid*' (French 2007: 160-161). In Poe's story, this scene has the character of a soliloquy; in the film, Philip is clearly present in the room, so Roderick's confession takes the form of a monologue. While Philip is the auditor, he remains out of shot and silent, which allows Roderick to take centre stage, giving the suggestion that his confession is aimed as much at the audience as Philip.

As in Poe's story, the revelation of Roderick's madness takes place with complete focus on Roderick. But since Roderick is not speaking to himself, but is addressing Philip, it would seem inappropriate for him to refer to himself as mad. So Matheson has Philip respond to Roderick's confession: 'you *are* mad' (French 2007: 161). The italics ask the actor to emphasise the verb, which Mark Damon does, making it Philip's final conclusion concerning Roderick's state of mind. Roderick may have gone mad, but the camera is focused on his tortured visage, forcing the audience to focus on Roderick. What is more, Madeline has been calling out for Roderick, not Philip. Like Poe's narrator, Philip has become a witness to a drama in which he plays no part. When Philip re-enters the frame, he attacks Roderick in furious tones. Only the noises signalling Madeline's escape from her casket, 'CRACKING, BREAKING, SPLINTERING' (2007: 164), distract him from his manhandling of Roderick. Deranged Roderick may be, but it is he, and not the staunch rationalist and increasingly aggressive Philip, who holds the viewers' attention and sympathy. Along with Roderick the audience now awaits his and Madeline's demise.

While Philip repeats his rushing about in frantic search of Madeline, Roderick remains passive in his hysteria, whispering only: '*she has the madness*' (French 2007: 167). Philip's search is anticlimactic; he fails to find his beloved. As he enters the gallery, the grotesque images of the evil Usher ancestors loom down on him, suggesting that it is not Madeline but he who is lost. In one of the few genuine jump scares in the picture, Madeline's bloody hand suddenly reaches out to Philip, dragging him to the floor. Not only does this original scene confirm Philip's impotence in the face of the Usher curse, it also confirms that Roderick was right all along in diagnosing Madeline with the Usher madness.

Parallel to Philip's frantic search, Matheson scripted another original scene in which Roderick grasps a pistol. Here Matheson seems to break with his sympathetic characterisation of Roderick, by suggesting he intends to murder his sister. Again, the audience is asked to provide their own motivation for this act. Does Roderick simply fear for his own life, or does he fear the consequences of Madeline's escape? In her madness, which gives her supernatural strength, Madeline could kill her brother and leave with Philip, leading to the prolongation of the Usher curse. From this perspective, Roderick's turn to a weapon makes sense. It dovetails with the explanations he has given Philip throughout the film. Roderick may be mad, and suffering in the grip of fear, but there is certainly method in his madness since a greater evil will be destroyed with the demise of his sister and himself, from his point of view.

Having failed to find Madeline anywhere in the house, and having been attacked by the house itself during the exposition, and by Madeline during the catastrophe, Philip must realise now that the house and its occupants are indeed one, indivisible and crumbling. In the final scene, Roderick, Philip and Madeline meet again in the same room in which they first encountered each other. This is an antiparallel to that scene. During the exposition, Roderick escorted Madeline away to her bedroom, and Philip was left standing alone in the living room, contemplating Roderick's prophetic painting of the house engulfed by flames. During the catastrophe, Madeline and Roderick, caught in a deadly struggle, are indeed consumed by the flames engulfing the room, as Bristol leads Philip away from the collapsing structure. As in Poe's original, the overall effect of the ambiguous catastrophe is that it leaves a receptive audience in a state of frightful wonder. Order has not been restored; in fact, all has been destroyed. But by what and to what purpose? Has the Usher curse struck at Roderick through Madeline because the former attempted to end the family's heritage of evil? Has Madeline avenged her mad brother's attempt at sororicide? Has Philip's intrusion into the House of Usher merely quickened its inevitable collapse? How strong an influence is family inheritance on the formation of individual personality; how dangerous is it to reject family tradition? Rich food to sustain the life of any teenager's thought.

CHAPTER 3: THE LOOK OF *USHER*: PICTURING A STORY OF DEATH

Unlike Poe, who was very much a solitary artist, Corman has always stressed the collaborative nature of film-making. Between 1954 and 1960, Corman assembled a group of artistic talents that he would later refer to as the 'Corman crew' (qtd in Naha 1982: 102). The two founding members of the crew were Corman himself in the role of producer/director, and the award-winning cinematographer Floyd Crosby, who worked on almost half of the pictures Corman made between 1954 and 1964. In 1958, Daniel Haller – a graduate of LA's Chouinard Art Institute – joined the crew as art director, working on most of Corman's films between 1958 and 1964. He would also direct films for AIP. Other long-term members of the Corman crew were set decorator Harry Reif, propmen Karl Brainard and Richard Rubin, editors Ronald Sinclair and Anthony Carras, composers Ronald Stein and Les Baxter, assistant director/production manager Jack Bohrer, Marjorie Corso of the costume and wardrobe department, key grip Charles Hanawalt and writers Charles B. Griffith and Mark Hanna. The Croman crew was most consistent between *War of the Satellites* (1958) and *The Haunted Palace* (1963) and very solid during the making of the first six Poe pictures. Responsible for the overall look of *House of Usher* were Crosby, Haller, Rubin, Reif and Corso. Together these artists developed the unique gothic aesthetics of AIP's Poe cycle that Tudor (1989: 55) and Aleksandrowicz (2016: 180) have likened to the expressionist horror tradition in cinematic art. The décor, as much as the dialogue, exudes the existential dread and the paradoxical feelings of fear and desire in the face of death so closely associated with Poe's angst-ridden tales of premature burial and spectral revelation.

It is true that the *mise-en-scène* of *House of Usher* dominates all but Vincent Price's powerful performance and has been instrumental to the film's cult status. In 1960, *Variety* foregrounded the film's aesthetics by noting that the 'aesthetic craftsmen' working on the picture 'tended almost to minimise the chilling story housed within their art' (qtd in Frank 1998: 91). Like Poe, Corman was taken more seriously in Europe than in his own country. As early as 1964 a retrospective of his films was organised at the *Cinématèque Française*. In 1970 (and again in 2009), the Edinburgh Film Festival held a Corman retrospective. In the early 1980s, Corman's Poe pictures received much praise in the German Retro *Filmprogramm* series, in which Winfried Günther described their lyrical quality. Corman's artistic credentials were raised in America when New York's MoMA organised a 25th anniversary American International retrospective, in 1979, which included a screening of *House of Usher*. In the first year of the twenty-first century, the Dutch Film Museum (now EYE Amsterdam) organised an event called *Macabre Nights: Roger Corman Meets Edgar Allan Poe*, screening all six of Corman's Poe pictures. The *NRC Handelsblad* described the films as dreamlike, containing a supernatural atmosphere, and an 'expressionistic' look that had a 'lightly hypnotic' effect on the audience. Bruce Lanier Wright has described *House of Usher* as 'elegant, drenched in atmosphere, and technically polished' with 'beautifully lit takes' composed of 'sinuous and evocative' camera work 'featuring unusual, disorienting angles and extensive use of point of view shots' and a 'stalking and gliding' camera that pulls the audience 'relentlessly through the house's brooding corridors' (1995: 114-5). *House of Usher* was an art film from the outset.

This sustained critical focus on the artistic value of Corman's Poe adaptations is not surprising since the film's director and its star shared an 'artful vision of Poe' (Price 1999: 217). In fact, as outlined in chapter one, Corman had quite an artful vision of film-making in general. Apart from employing his usual crew, Corman approached various recognised artistic talents within the industry whenever he felt he could use their input. When Crosby was not available, for instance, he enrolled *Bride of Frankenstein*'s (1935) John J. Mescall into his crew to shoot *Not of this Earth*. He also employed Looney Tunes' legend Paul Julian to create evocative title sequences for some of his films. As a result, Corman's pictures often look much better than their budgets would suggest. The *mise-en-scene* is often fully integrated into the story, expressive of its major themes, and evoking and sustaining the right mood.

Take *War of the Satellites*, for instance, the first picture on which Haller, Crosby, Corso, Brainard and Reiff worked together. The sets, costumes, shapes, shades, frame-composition and camera angles all combine to foreground the central themes of science losing control in its confrontation with the ultimate unknown, and the polarisation of communities through fear. The central location during the first half of the picture is an aerospace research and control centre. Almost everything, from the rooms, hallways, windows, furniture and technical apparatus is rectangular in shape.

Figs. 7–9 War of the Satellites

The circular objects that stand out amongst all the straight lines and hard edges are the telescope, the satellite and the model rockets and other rocket-shaped objects strategically placed in the background. Such an organised contrast between angular and circular shapes enables the sets to become expressive of a central thematic dichotomy in the story: the law and order of human science will be confronted by the unmeasurable infinity of space. In the still above, the shape-shifting alien, having taken on the guise of Dr Pol van Ponder, is communicating with his fellow aliens. The coming together, on the one hand, of the angular shapes of the desk, the apparatus, the picture on the wall and the panelling, and, on the other hand, the misty vortex representing the alien presence and the rocket-shaped props on the cabinet, express the coming together of two worlds, as embodied by the possessed figure of Van Ponder. There are obvious patterns in the design of *War of the Satellites* that foreground the themes of breaking barriers, confrontation, and mirroring that reinforce the picture's message that science is a double-edged sword. Notably, when the protagonists travel into space, there is a predominance of curved shapes. The curved rocketship interiors not only create a contrast between the straight lines of the angular space station sets; they also give the claustrophic rocket sets a true sense of depth. In doing so these sets continue the spiral designs present at various key moments of the film that give expression to the mysterious infinitude of space. The constant repetition of circular patterns in space graphically represents the danger of straddling the boundaries of a vortex that has the power to pull everything into its destructive centre.

This chapter will analyse the artistic aspects of *House of Usher* to reveal that the Corman crew managed to successfully fuse the dark Romantic tradition to which Poe belongs with a more expressionist horror film aesthetic that made the film more directly appealing to 1960s horror-movie audiences. Used in the context of low-budget horror films, expressionism should be understood as a term denoting 'art which depends on free and obvious distortions of natural forms to convey emotional feeling' (Baur 1951: 5). *House of Usher* is not expressionistic because its frames resemble the art of Edvard Munch, or *Die Brücke*, but because its *mise-en-scène* is not naturalistic but functions as a visual vehicle for the expression of subjective states of mind and emotions. In developing *House of Usher*, Corman told his crew: 'I never want to see "reality" in any of these scenes' (1998: 81). The décor of the Usher mansion is not designed for verisimilitude, but to give the audience a glimpse at the fear that lurks in the darkest corners of Roderick's psyche.

MATTE ROMANTICISM

Many atmospheric descriptors have been used over the years to describe the ambiance of *House of Usher*: dreamlike, supernatural, brooding. One of the most unique and ubiquitous aspects of Poe's art is his skill in using words to construct striking mental pictures of dreamscapes pervaded by a mysteriously moribund atmosphere evocative of a spirit world. In one of his early poems, Poe wrote of the 'vivid colouring' of dreams that contrasted with 'the dull reality of waking life' (2000: 68-9). Many of Poe's poems are visionary in this way, expressing in strange figural compositions and landscapes the fear of death and the desire to know what lies beyond the threshold of life. In Poe's early lyric 'The Lake', for example, the speaker reminisces on the delightful terror he experienced while haunting the shores of a desolate spot, 'a feeling undefin'd, / Springing from a darken'd mind' (*Complete Poems* 2000: 85). Similarly, the speaker in 'The Sleeper' invokes a midnight graveyard in which 'The rosemary nods upon the grave; / The lilly lolls upon the wave; / Wrapping the fog about its breast', as 'The ruin moulders into rest' (*Complete Poems* 2000: 187). In 'The City in the Sea', a personification of 'Death looks gigantically down' on a world where 'open fanes and gaping graves / Yawn level with the luminous waves' (*Complete Poems* 2000: 202). Much of Poe's writing is characterised by this morbid fascination with the world beyond the boundary of life, as the discussion of 'Dream-land' in chapter one also revealed.

As a writer, Poe belonged to the anti-mimetic Romantic tradition that utilised the imagery of ruins, graveyards and bleak natural scenes to create symbolic landscapes invoking the contemplation of what H.G. Schenk has termed 'the anguish of the void' (1966: 53). This makes Poe's nightmarish dreamscapes, as well as Roderick Usher's artworks, poetic versions of Caspar David Friedrich's dark Romantic 'deathscapes' as Karl Whittington calls them. For Friedrich 'artistic expression was about rendering visible the interior self' (Whittington 2012). Many of his landscapes, like Poe's writings, and Roderick Usher's works of art, are symbolic in this way. They are expressive of states of consciousness, deeply felt inner moods and intuitions of a spirit world that exists beyond the reach of our bodily senses. Where eighteenth-century graveyard poetry sought to express similar visions from within a traditional Christian framework of hope and salvation, Poe's brand of dark Romanticism echoes Friedrich's in doing away with the hopeful appeal to spiritual transcendence. It primarily gives expression to the anxiety, fear and bewilderment experienced by the visionary who imaginatively confronts death and finds it simultaneously an insoluble mystery fraught with terror and a source of relief, what Schenk calls 'an everlasting general anaesthesia, an insensibility to all kinds of pain and suffering' (1966: 63). The landscape Philip Winthrop enters in Corman's *House of Usher* should be understood as such a darkly Romantic symbolic region.

In Poe's story, the domain is characterised by 'a black and lurid tarn' surrounded by grey and 'rank sedges' (2000: 397) and 'ghastly tree-stems' (2000: 398). The house is characterised by its 'vacant eye-like windows' and 'bleak walls' (2000: 397) that, while solid, comprised of 'crumbling' (2000: 400) stones. The whole was overspread with 'minute fungi'; a 'barely perceptible fissure' ran 'in a zigzag direction' from the roof into the tarn, and 'a pestilent and mystic vapor, sluggish, faintly discernible, and leaden hued' (ibid.) enveloped all. As discussed in chapter two, all these details allow Poe to construct his allegory of a mind in an advanced state of decay; a man outwardly living, but dying inside, whose art reveals a fearful vision of the dark mysteries that await.

Caspar David Friedrich's 'The Abbey in the Oak Wood' (1809-10) is one of the most iconic and most-often reproduced Romantic deathscapes. In his discussion of the various interpretations of this artwork, Whittington points out that 'Quite simply put, the Abbey is a depressing painting'. According to Whittington, interpretations of the painting that emphasise a positive spiritual transcendence – a heavenly afterlife – ignore its overall mood: 'the fear of death, of its vastness and depth, is just barely managed by placing the scene within a decaying yet somehow attractive other world – a ruined medieval church'. He emphasises that photographic reproductions of the painting have only distorted viewers' understanding of it because in the original 'there truly is not a single warm color … only washed-out grays, blacks, browns, and whites'. According to Whittington, the 'otherworldly' light 'transports the viewer into another time and space' in which 'the dead lie decaying and forgotten along with the church, both relics offering not consolation or completion, but stifling stillness and the creeping destruction of time and neglect'. As an elaborate *memento mori* landscape, this iconic image of German Romanticism 'expresses exactly this sense of the unspeakable fear surrounding death', by leaving 'obscure what lies beyond the barrier' (Whittington 2012). 'The Fall of the House of Usher' is a literary work that expresses this dark Romantic malaise of the soul through verbal rather than pictorial symbolism. Fittingly, Friedrich's 'Abbey' was used by Naxos as the cover for an audiobook titled *The Fall of the House of Usher, The Pit and the Pendulum and Other Tales of Mystery and Imagination* (2003).

Fig. 10 'The Abbey in the Oak Wood'

The opening sequence of *House of Usher*, reveals the extent to which Corman's crew was clearly inspired by the Romantic deathscape tradition, if not directly by Friedrich's ruined abbey. Corman has explained that the opening shot of Philip Winthrop riding through 'a very desolate landscape' was filmed in a part of the Hollywood Hills destroyed by fire (qtd in Naha 1982: 31). The atmosphere of decay that this image of natural destruction portrays is meant to set the tone of the entire picture and is symbolic of the major theme of Poe's tale: man's simultaneous fear of and fascination with death. It is reprised during the flashback scene when Roderick explains the coming of the Usher plague. The matte paining of the house resembles Friedrich's masterpiece in both colour and composition.

Fig. 11 The house

The same shades of brown and grey dominate the image and the mist-enshrouded central structure seems to rise into a luminescent sky. The low-angle from which the image is rendered, and the lack of any recognisable geographical referents in the scene, give the impression that the building is floating in mid-air, stifling any potential for verisimilitude and enhancing the symbolic potential of the picture as a deathscape. As Philip rides through the gate, the crumbling garden wall, the hollow tree trunk and the crumbling exterior of the house all signal that he is entering a dying world.

When the matte painting of the Usher mansion is contrasted with the one establishing the setting of *The Pit and the Pendulum*, the extent to which the former exudes doom and decay becomes apparent.

Fig. 12 The Pit and the Pendulum

Fig. 13 'View of Tantallon Castle and the Bass Rock'

In the opening sequence of *Pit*, the production team builds on the more traditionally Romantic sublime image of the cliff-edge castle, as exemplified by Alexander Nasmyth's 'View of Tantallon Castle and the Bass Rock' (1816). Such sublime scenes evoke a sense of awe in mankind's helplessness against the destructive power of nature, as well as nature's powerful beauty. The strong contrasts between light and shade and the clearly demarcated boundaries between earth, sea and sky, situate the narrative in a world fully recognisable as our own, if emotionally enhanced through the dramatic use of light, shade and perspective. A key contrast between *Usher*'s and *Pit*'s establishing matte shots is that between the floating image of the house and the firmly grounded castle. While Francis Barnard is clearly travelling somewhere, to a place in space and time (however bleak), Philip Winthrop enters a mysterious misty region that shares with Friedrich's painting a 'cold isolation and a nightmarish non-reality' (Whittington 2012). On the inside, Don Medina's castle contains a terrible torture chamber. The threat in *Pit* is unambiguously real and man-made. The House of Medina is destroyed by the corrupting forces of lust and a will to power. The House of Usher, by contrast, contains only a crypt, and legends of ancestral evil; it is a symbolic structure, expressive of the angst dominating the mind of its protagonist.

The final matte painting in *House of Usher* once again follows Friedrich's technique of 'silhouetting [a] foreground image against an intangible background' (Vaughan et.al. 1972: 30).

Fig. 14 The ruins of Usher

Fig. 15 'Winter'

Notably, all colour has been drained from the image, which is dominated by the grey mist engulfing the black ruins of the mansion and the trees. Like Friedrich's 'Winter' (1808), the painting emenates decay in every aspect. While Friedrich's bleak landscape is still inhabited by a solitary figure struggling through the snow, the film's final image is literally lifeless. The House of Usher, which had been an imposing presence in the establishing matte painting, is now imposed upon by the ominous skyscape that pushes the ruins down into the mist. This final dark Romantic image of death allows the audience to forget Philip Winthrop almost immediately and to leave the theatre brooding over the fate of the Ushers and the accuracy of Roderick's vision. Of course, the audience would not consciously associate the final image in the film with Friedrich's 'Winter'. But that is not the point. These images share a very specific aesthetic, expressive of a major dark Romantic spiritual theme that foreshowed the more modern exisistential angst about the ultimate mystery of what lies beyond the threshold, and how this can hollow out the meaningfulness of life on the vital side of death.

MEMENTO MORI AND VANITAS

Another artistic tradition from which the Corman crew drew inspiration was that of the memento mori and vanitas still-lifes of the seventeenth century. Throughout the film, various props inside the house function as memento mori. Crosby's camera lingers long enough on the hourglass on the table in Philip's room, the open bible underneath a crucifix in the chapel and the cobweb-covered skeleton of one of the Usher ancestors to turn these frames into still-lifes symbolic of the transience of human existence. When these traditional memento mori images are combined with candles, books, musical instruments, globes and painting utensils (also present in Epstein's 1928 adaptation), the resulting frames come to resemble the more elaborate vanitas still-lifes that remind the onlooker of the transience of human life and the ultimate vanity (in the sense of worthlessness or moral emptiness) of material possessions, sensual delights and bookish learning.

Roderick is often seen playing his lute, an instrument often found in vanitas paintings because, on the one hand, the lute was considered 'the Queen of musical instruments', but, on the other hand, music was considered 'typically a transient form of art: as soon as the sound has died away, the composition no longer exists' (Burgers 2013: 198; 201). The sets in House of Usher are decorated throughout with red candles. A candle is the symbol for the human soul in vanitas paintings. In the film, the candles are strategically placed to complement Roderick's metaphor that he and his sister are 'two pale drops of fire guttering in the vast, consuming darkness' (French 2007: 73). In one shot, at the dinner table, a close-up of Philip shows him sandwiched between two burning candles of equal length. In the after-dinner scene the candles not only highlight the 'deep composition' (Aleksandrowicz 2016: 175) that draws the viewer into the room, as if sitting opposite Roderick at the table, but their strategic placement also has great

Fig. 16 *Still life*

Fig. 17 *Vanitas*

Fig. 18 *Symbolic candles*

symbolic potential. The placement of the candles creates a spatial boundary that divides Philip from Roderick, with Madeline exactly on the dividing line.

Moreover, the flame on the shortest candle, the one closest to Madeline, has died out before the wax has burnt up. Later, when Madeline has supposedly died, Roderick lights a single candle in a hurricane candle holder – symbolic of the storm he knows he will soon have to face head on – and reflects in a melancholy tone, 'one candle left to burn now'. The *vanitas* aspect of the above frame is further enhanced by the globe behind Roderick. When combined with other *vanitas* props a globe signifies 'the world's transient nature' (Mokre 2000: 9). Throughout the film, Roderick is surrounded

Fig. 19 Roderick and his props

by vanitas props – his lute, his painting instruments, candles – as if his art constitutes his existence and both are worthless.

Roderick's complete immersion in his art suggests also that he believes in the aphorism 'life is short / art is long'. It is his creativity that is keeping him alive, although the broken notes from his lute after dinner and his phantasmagorical paintings suggest that he is also losing control of his talents and has become incapable as an artist of perceiving and recording the beauty and harmony of the world. Roderick's music and pictures tell the story of his and Madeline's broken lives at the House of Usher.

VISUAL STORYTELLING

While Roderick's art expresses what he cannot put into words, Corman and his team were also adept at allowing the visuals to carry much of the emotional content of their films. Already in the 1950s the Corman crew persistently drew their audiences into the world of the movie by means of expressive, high-tension title sequences that set the tone for the picture. The opening of *Machine Gun Kelly* perfectly illustrates Corman's penchant for visual story-telling. A loud drumroll announces the AIP logo, which in turn sets off an energetic big-band jazz theme over Bill Martin's cartoon graphics that introduce the key elements of the film: criminals, guns, cash and cars. Music and image are synchronised as each drum- and horn-break in the music is graphically represented by the appearance of a bullet hole on the screen.

The smooth edit from the title sequence to the first scene is accompanied by a similarly smooth change of mood in the music, from kinetic horns to a low-key, piano-driven theme, echoed by melancholy notes on wind instruments. While the musical shift in tone helps to raise curiosity, it also functions as a prelude for the explosive exposition

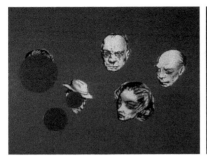

Figs. 20–21 Machine Gun Kelly

that follows: a six-minute action-packed instrumental number in which the main characters and action are introduced through purely visual storytelling techniques. The crime committed is shown through a shadow play, and the protagonists are introduced to the audience as they race through the countryside, ditching their disguises and the loot in order to disperse. An energetic jazz number drives up the tension as well as the thrills. Only when the protagonist limps toward his female accomplice, waiting in a car at a rendezvous point, does the band mellow out. The first words in the film are spoken by Flo to Kelly: 'Did you have a good time honey?' (0:06:04). She may well be asking the audience: 'How do you like it so far?'

In the opening sequence of *House of Usher* the Corman crew once again used visual story-telling techniques to introduce the audience to the film's central theme: death. This time, figural animation has been replaced with abstract visuals that achieve communication between artwork and audience through shape and colour alone. Ward Preston points out that the 'emotional associations [that colours invoke] constitute a universal language that can be exploited by the sensitive designer' (1994: 75). *House of Usher* opens with a purple mist swirling over a pitch-black screen, enveloping the white letters of the title sequence. The mist changes its hews from purple to blue, to green, back to purple, to red, to purple again and back to blue before fading out.

In 1949, the psychologist B.J. Kouwer published his phenomenological study of the experience of colour, in which he explained in great detail how colours work expressively to generate specific feelings and connotations in human beings. Black and

James H. Nicholson & Samuel Z. Arkoff
PRESENT

Fig 22 Opening sequence

purple he found were universally experienced as colours with macabre overtones. Black was (unsurprisingly) associated with death, murder, anxiety, misery, and the night (1949: 81-2). 'In the color black', he explained, 'we experience the Nought', the existential void, 'although we cannot see it as such' (1949: 89). Black represents the 'unknown'; it is 'endless, empty, silent, deep' (ibid.). As a consequence it effects our mood making us feel 'sad, somber, depress[ed], gloomy, sorrowful, miser[able]' (1949: 92), depending on the context. Purple was considered 'unreliable, disharmonious, dubious, perverse, hypocritical, unbalanced, ambivalent, good and bad at the same time, favourable and unfavourable, attractive and repulsive' (1949: 128). Depending on the context, blue was considered 'modest', 'unpretentious', 'unobtrusive', holding connotations of 'vastness', 'endlessness', the 'ideal', and 'melancholy' (1949: 115-6). It could also communicate 'the repression of emotional intensity', coldness, arrogance and aggression (1949: 121). Red was ubiquitously experienced as 'the color of vitality' and passion (1949: 104-6); Green (unsurprisingly) was associated with nature and youth, but also with poison and deceit, depending on the context (1949: 124-136).

In *House of Usher*, Corman made full use of the symbolic potential of colour. The predominantly purple hews on a black background work well to set an ominous mood at the outset, which is further enhanced when the swirling coloured mist of the title sequence becomes the lingering grey fog of the opening scene, in which the blackness is transposed to the dead tree branches through which Philip makes his way to the mansion. The dominant palette in the opening scene comprises of shades of grey, black and rusty brown, colours of lifelessness and decay. Philip's dark blue overcoat stands in contrast to the scenery, suggesting that he does not belong. On his entrance into the house he seems calm and collected, but as the analysis of the screenplay in chapter 2 has revealed, this level-headed outward appearance masks repressed emotions that surface and eventually run amok when he finally manages to lay his blue jacket aside.

Roderick is initially dressed in a long bright red gown. Kouwer explains that 'red dominates everything around it, touching and consuming it in its glow' (1949: 102). Price's character is certainly a domineering presence from the outset. But his gown also hides his inner self. It seems strange that a figure so obsessed with death would wear a gown the colour of which symbolises life and passion. But Kouwer explains that, in relation to death, the life affirming and energetic qualities of red give it the potential to function as 'a protection from and defense against evil influences' (1949: 104). Madeline also wears a red dress in the evening. The candles in the house are also red, but of course the flame is ever consuming the wax. In the film red represents the fuel of life, a fuel that is consumed to stay alive. The candles light the dark house, the characters drink wine from red glasses, and the fire keeps them warm. But as Usher's painting of the house foreshadows, it will ultimately consume their lives.

The morning after Philip's arrival, Madeline has exchanged her red dress for a grey one. According to Kouwer's research 'gray is nothing, neither good nor bad … passively it yields to outside influence' (1949: 135-6). It is in this garment that Madeline leads Philip down into the Usher vaults to persuade him of the inevitability of her doom. Meanwhile, Roderick has changed into a black suit with a dark red waistcoat, suggesting that his lifeblood is also ebbing away fast. Convinced of the inevitability of Madeline's demise, Roderick may have donned this mourning garb in foresight. Philip, refusing to acknowledge Roderick's and Madeline's perspective, still wears his blue suit. The near absence of white in the *mise-en-scène* or costuming (apart from Bristol's and Philips's shirts and the candles in the chapel) suggests that the House of Usher is indeed a domain tainted with evil. Kouwer explains that white predominantly symbolises 'purity' in particular 'freedom from sin' (1949: 97). Significantly, Madeline is buried in a light pink, rather than a pure white gown, suggesting that, like her brother, she is tainted by the Usher lineage. But the delicate pink hue also suggests that there is still a trace of life flowing through her body, which is confirmed when her fingers are shown to tremble ever so slightly. The Corman crew must have deliberated carefully on the film's palette, as the colours used perfectly underscore the personalities of the three main characters, their relation towards each other and their role in the central drama.

Not only colour, also 'texture' (Preston 1994: 81) is important in establishing the overall mood of a film. Surfaces can be rough or smooth, broken or seamless, colours can be flat or glossy, and sets can be brightly lit or engulfed by shadow; background props can be kinetic or statuesque (Preston 1994: 81-84). One of the great qualities of *House of Usher* is the overall texture of the frames, a stylistic quality that unites most of the AIP Poe pictures. It is a fundamentally moribund texture created by the chiaroscuro lighting effects and the elaborately carved dark wood furniture and statues, walls hung with rich drapes and heavy cobwebs. It is a paradoxical texture of velvet grotesquery, like a rotting but moss-overgrown tree trunk. The colour schemes and texture of *House of Usher* also echo the look of the gothic stories in EC horror comics, a visual story-telling language with which many older teenagers may well have been familiar in 1960. 'The Curse of Harkley Heath', from *Vault of Horror* 13 (1950), is a re-imagining of Poe's 'The Fall of the House of Usher'. Remarkably, it contains panels that appear almost verbatim in Corman's film but which are not in Poe's original story. In one panel, a chandelier falls from the ceiling (in this case on the murderous villain of the story). The climactic scene resembles Corman's also. The victimised heroine returns from the grave in search of vengeance on her family, whilst a fire destroys the mansion. The final panels are that of a woman's face in the flames and a sinking ruin, just as in Corman's film.

USHER'S / SHONBERG'S ART

One of the most genuinely expressionistic aspects of *House of Usher* is Roderick Usher's art, as well as the portraits of his family, that seem not to have been painted by Roderick, as their style is less abstract, but no less expressionistic. These artworks were created by Burt Shonberg, a Los Angeles artist and illustrator who in 1957 had 'dramatic experiences beyond the limits of so-called ordinary, everyday consciousness'. These transcendental phenomena revealed to him 'the undeniable truth of our situation in ordinary worldly life'. Unfortunately, these revelations were 'so frightfully staggering' that he initially reacted in 'stark terror' (Shonberg 2009). Soon, however, he learned to embrace them as an unorthodox source of wisdom. Strikingly, in his memoir 'Out Here', Shonberg's descriptions of his transcendent experiences echo Poe's descriptions of dream-land. He explains that 'there was no such thing as inside any more' and that he found himself 'outside of moving time' (ibid.). Corman understood Poe as an artist who 'probed the farthest reaches of the mind' (BFI 2013). Marshall Berle, curator

of Shonberg's website, has described the artist as 'a prospector of consciousness';
like Poe's speculative tales, his artworks are 'journeys to the outer edges of human
perception' (Alfonso 2015). More than a century apart, Shonberg and Poe shared a
desire to expand the vistas of human consciousness and were not afraid to journey
into the shadows to achieve their aim. By the time Corman was developing *House of
Usher*, Shonberg had been art director on AIP's paranoid SF thriller *The Brain Eaters*
(1958) and had contributed artwork to various science fiction magazines. He was
also co-proprietor of the bohemian art-hangout Café Frankenstein, in Laguna Beach,
together with science fiction author George Clayton Johnson and folk musician Doug
Myres (of the Gateway Singers). This background made Shonberg the perfect artist to
produce Roderick Usher's paintings. Spencer Kansa explains that 'having seen marvellous
examples of' Shonberg's art 'in the coffeehouses on the Strip', Corman 'hired him
to create the ancestral portraits that hang in the Usher mansion, confident he could
convey the evil inherent in the faces depicted' (2017: 77).

Matheson included a description of the painting of the house into his original script:
'a brooding impressionistic study of the house which conveys more vividly the aura
of corrupt decay which we have only sensed in seeing the house itself' (French 2007:
68). Shonberg probably understood what Matheson really wanted: a picture that
expressed the overall atmosphere of dread and decay in the House of Usher. Seen
from a distance, as Philip initially does, the picture is dominated by the bright-red orb
above the mansion. Audience members familiar with the story, will immediately associate
the painting with the narrator's observation of a 'full, setting, and blood-red moon,
which now shone vividly through that once barely-discernible fissure' (Poe 2000: 417).
Within the context of Roderick's deep studies in mystical prophecy and the nature
of the spirit world, the blood-red moon appearing at the catastrophe alludes to the
biblical prophecy in Joel that speaks of how 'the sun shall be turned into darkness, and
the moon into blood, before the great and terrible day of the Lord come' (2:31). It is
a sign that the inevitable apocalypse has arrived. A close-up of the painting reveals that
the red orb is repeated in the structure of the house, which consists almost entirely of
spherical and triangular shapes in red, orange and yellow tints, surrounded by swirls of
salmon-coloured smoke pierced by flickerings of a silver-blue light. As briefly discussed in
chapter two, this painting foreshadows the catastrophe of the film, just as the allegorical

ballad 'The Haunted Palace' foreshadows Roderick's fate in Poe's story. Roderick knows the catastrophe that awaits, but is only able to express this knowledge through his art initially, as putting it into words – as Philip forces him to do eventually – is too confrontational.

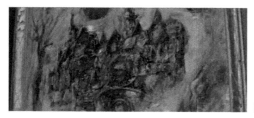

Fig. 23 Shonberg's 'House of Usher'

This ability of expressionistic art to reveal the 'repressed aspects of the psyche' (Bassie 2008: 51) is masterfully rendered in Shonberg's portraits of the Usher ancestors. In terms of portrait painting, Oskar Kokoschka was the expressionist most talented in 'revealing the inner nature of his sitters' (Bassie 2008: 60). Kokoschka's technique was described as a form of 'X-ray vision', which allowed him 'not only to see the "true" inner nature of his sitters, but their past and even their future too' (Bassie 2008: 65). An understanding of the creative artist as a visionary is not typical of expressionism alone. It was also very much a trope in the Romantic age. In *The House of the Seven Gables* (1851), Nathaniel Hawthorne suggested that the new-fangled daguerreotype technique, in the hands of the artist Holgrave, had the power to reveal inner corruption hiding behind a façade of respectability. Poe's 'House of Usher' was a definite inspiration for Hawthorne. His Pyncheon family, like the Ushers, are cursed by ancestral abuse of power and privilege. It is in its laying bare of inner corruption that the dark Romantic mode of Poe and Hawthorne dovetails with the expressionist art of the first half of the twentieth century, which foregrounded 'what was unruly violent, chaotic, ecstatic or even demonic' (Bassie 2008: 51) in the human character. In Corman's film, Shonberg's portraits of the Usher ancestors illustrate Roderick's monologue detailing the criminal, debauched and outright evil actions of his ancestors. What unifies the pictures is the dark, cold and hollow stare of the eyes, deeply set in a spectral-white or glowing-red cadaverous visage. The alternating pale and fiery hues of the portraits give the impression that the Ushers dwelt either in utter darkness or in a burning hell.

Figs. 24–26 Shonberg's Usher portraits

One of the most evocative frames in the picture, one that signals the catastrophe, brings Roderick, his art, and his sister together in a unified image expressive of the fear that has haunted the protagonists throughout. Roderick's portrait of Madeline contains the same basic shapes, colour palette and brush-stroke technique as his picture of the house; only the distribution of circular and triangular shapes, and red, yellow and topaz-blue is different. Not only does this reveal that the images were created by the same artistic imagination; it solidifies the link between the house and its inhabitants. They are made of the same materials, and infused with the same spirit. But while the house is characterised by the flaming red and yellow brushstrokes that constitute its gables, and is enshrouded by a misty haze of blueish grey pierced by a blood-red sun, the portrait of Madeline, while drawn with the same dark stare and a similar facial features as her evil ancestors, is surrounded not by a shadowy or fiery background, but by a swirling blue chaos, dappled with red and yellow streaks. In the lightening that illuminates the portrait during the catastrophe, the blue hues are foregrounded; in the close-up with Roderick,

Fig. 27 Roderick's Madeline

the colours infect even Usher's pale visage, drawing him into the picture and foreshadowing the unavoidable dissolution of the siblings. According to Kouwer, in its positive connotations 'blue stands for man's spiritual aspirations, his strife toward the absolute' (1949: 119). In this light, blue 'represents morality in its human altruistic, self-sacrificing function' (1949: 120). In its more negative connotations it can represent 'repression of emotional intensity' and can become 'the color of puritanism, of the condemnation and negation of corporeity' (1949: 120-1). Roderick may have painted Madeline in hues of topaz blue because he believed that in sacrificing himself and his sister for the good of mankind (by ending the Usher curse) he would achieve his highest spirtitual goal; but in doing so, Roderick also denied Madeline her own will, and her own desires, revealing his own lack of emotional warmth. By facing his portrait of Madeline at the catastrophe, Roderick is finally coming face to face with his own deepest fears: that in achieving what he believed to be the ultimate act of altruism, he has in fact committed the crime of sororicide. *House of Usher* is a fantastic tale, and Roderick and Madeline are two fantastic figures, symbolic of the two halves of a single psyche; the part that knows, fears but calmly waits and the part that feels, believes and rebels against fate. Neither one can be heroic or villainous, as both are only half of consciousness. Self-knowledge for Roderick comes with wholeness of mind, which means recognising his own 'sinful' nature and experiencing guilt and remorse: a fearful prospect for any adolescent leaving the cinema after the House of Usher has collapsed in flames.

CHAPTER 4: THE USHER SIBLINGS: REBELS WITHOUT A CHANCE

Samuel J. Arkoff has argued that in the early 1950s no one in the movie industry was taking care of the teenagers (Arkoff 1991: 06:16). AIP jumped into this gap in the market and made films that often presented the world from a teenage perspective by including protagonists, themes and music that tied in seamlessly with the youth culture of the day. According to Thomas Doherty 'the best of them, like *I was a Teenage Werewolf*, show genuine insight into the inner life of their target audience' (2002: 132). This chapter will explore the characterisation of Roderick and Madeline in *House of Usher* as inheritors of a pernicious family legacy to which the brother responds in angst and the sister in anger.

If you are wondering how teenagers could be expected to identify with a middle-aged protagonist completely alienated from society, imprisoned in the family mansion, scared to distraction of his inheritance, and totally ineffective in warding off the impending doom, Paul Goodman's *Growing Up Absurd* (1960) can provide some answers. Goodman explains that youngsters in the 1950s were confronted with a world of 'stifling conformity' (1960: ix), in which politics and business were intricately related (1960: x) to form a fully 'organized society' in which institutions such as the family, education and mass media socialised the individual into accepting the dominant ideology as objective truth. He explains that the rise in so-called juvenile delinquency and the increasingly vocal dissent against the dominant ideology in the 1950s may not be down to faults within the socialising institutions, but may be down to the fact that 'the social message … communicated clearly to the young men [and women] … is unacceptable' (1960: 11). Boys and girls were given a difficult choice: 'either one drifts with [the grown-ups'] absurd system of ideas, believing that this is the human community. Or one dissents totally from their system of ideas and stands as a lonely human being' (1960: 134).

For Goodman the Beats were a prime example of a dissenting subculture, a group of young adults 'who have resigned from the organized system of production and sales and its culture, and yet who are too hip to be attracted to independent work' (1960: 170). By resigning 'from the rat race, they have removed the block' that stifled their creativity and devote themselves to the arts 'honestly, with earnest absorption', which 'sharpens the perceptions, releases and refines feelings, and is a powerful community bond' (1960: 176). The Beat culture's artistic endeavour is one of 'personal cultivation … its aim is action and self-expression and not the creation of culture and value or making a difference in the further world' (ibid.). Goodman's analysis of Beat culture suggests a dissent through conscious withdrawal from mainstream society and the socialised self and a recreation of a more authentic identity through artistic self-expression. It suggests that valid knowledge about self and society can be found by employing the creative imagination, rather than scientific rationalism or formal logic.

Vincent Price's Roderick Usher, to a large extent, conforms to the stereotype of the artist (like Shonberg) whose visionary imagination has given him an intuitive grasp of evil and profound knowledge of the future on which he has to act, while his skill and insight has simultaneously alienated him from society altogether, placing him in a position in which taking action becomes futile. Roderick is convinced that 'evil is not just a word … it is a reality' (0:40:42), a social reality that cannot be measured by statistics, defined by laws and policed by institutions because it spreads like a disease 'malignant, cancerous' (0:42:13). It can only be eradicated by destroying the corrupted matter on which it feeds: the Usher family. Madeline is similarly trapped in the Usher mansion, and, like her brother, a victim of her family's evil heritage; doubly a victim, as her brother plans to end the curse by sacrificing them both.

ANGST: VINCENT PRICE'S RODERICK

According to Corman, Roderick Usher is 'an extremely intelligent, extremely sensitive and very complex person' (qtd in Price 1999: 212). He is nothing like Peter Cushing's cruel and calculating Victor Frankenstein, or Christopher Lee's aggressively seductive Count Dracula. Matheson agreed with Corman and characterised Roderick as 'handsome' and 'talented'. He is a 'mystic' who 'believes, completely, in the curse of the Ushers'. While 'he does not shrink from personal death … he believes that [the] after-life offers him no more than continued suffering. Nor does he wish to hurt his sister for he loves her very much – so much, indeed, that he feels every pang of suffering she does' (French 2007: 52).

This is the characterisation of Roderick Usher from which Price developed his role. His own understanding of Roderick dovetailed with Corman's and Matheson's: 'I loved the white-haired character I was playing', he explained 'because he is the most sensitive of all Poe's heroes' (qtd in Price 1999: 212). Price's use of the word hero to describe Roderick Usher is significant. It reveals something about the actor's general understanding of Poe's protagonists. The classic hero performs daring, valiant and altruistic actions in 'a cause outside of himself' (Furst 1976: 56). While many mainstream Hollywood heroes embody this traditional template, the post-war period saw a rise in popularity of the anti-hero in both literary fiction and popular film: a taciturn, troubled, lonely individual caught up in a social web of intrigue from which he must untangle himself in order to fulfil a more personal existential quest. This often morally ambivalent protagonist, whose words and actions are subversive of received cultural traditions, was a post-war reimagining of the Romantic heroes that peopled Poe's tales. Lilian Furst explains that such Romantic heroes were predominantly concerned with their own psyche:

> The proud awareness of himself – rightly or wrongly – as an exceptional being leads to a cultivation of his differentness and to a constantly renewed brooding on his state to a depth of self-involution where his introverted sense of self completely distorts his perception of outer reality with the result that he goes on to sink even further into himself. (1976: 57)

Roderick Usher, as portrayed by Vincent Price in Corman's *House of Usher*, if not in Poe's allegorical tale, is a Romantic or anti-hero of this type.

According to his daughter Victoria, Price was able to deliver such a persuasive performance as Roderick because he 'had an affinity with Poe's characters. He was attracted to the Romantic ethos of these Gothic tales, in which hypersensitive men whose dark heritage combined with their refined sensibilities, doomed them to torment as outsiders' (Price 1999: 212). When Price agreed to play the part of Poe's famous Romantic misfit, his most recent notable roles had been the bewildered Francois Delambre in *The Fly* (1957), the acerbic millionaire Frederick Loren in William Castle's fun-filled *House on Haunted Hill* (1958), and the obsessed scientist Warren Chapin in *The Tingler* (1959). While these three films are all hilarious shockers, the characters Price played are neither heroic nor villainous. Delambre is very understanding but mostly clueless. As a house party host, Loren's dry cynicism is part of his charm. Chapin is a tragic science fiction hero, whose potentially world-changing discovery comes at too great a cost. Price had shown in these films that he could be simultaneously helpless and persevering, sinister and charismatic, angst-ridden and philosophical, making him the perfect actor to embody Poe's reclusive, visionary artist Roderick Usher. In fact, by turning to Usher, Price could perfect the persona of the self-absorbed and wronged creative genius he had initially cultivated with great success in *House of Wax* (1953) and had further developed in *The Mad Magician* (1954).

Ward Preston explains that a good art director will 'study the personalities of the scripted characters and wrap a life around them' (1994: 33). Close scrutiny of Roderick's drawing room reveals much about his personality. It becomes apparent that Roderick Usher is a multi-talented artist. Not only does he play the lute and paint, his house is filled with antique as well as more contemporary statues, paintings, intricately carved pieces of furtinure and delicate glass ware.

Fig. 28 The drawing room

Usher's drawing room looks like a gothic version of Price's own, judging by the publicity photos for *I Like What I Know*, Price's book about his 'long-time love-affair' (1959: 244) with art. Vincent Price had been an art-lover from his teenage years, touring European museums at sixteen, trying his own hand at art and eventually becoming a student of art-history at Yale (Price 1959: 41-90). By the 1950s the actor had become both a serious collector and popular lecturer on art. Next to being a devotee of painting, Price was known to produce poetry 'on the back of deli menus, custom receipts, and bank deposit slips, on hotel stationary from around the world, on movie call sheets, and on reams of lined notebook paper' (Williams 1998: 33). Price believed that great works of art had the potential to 'purify the materialistic smog of America' (1959: 75). For Price, art was spiritual and non-obtrusively didactic: 'it teaches you ... tolerance. And more than tolerance ... understanding' (1959: 64). Moreover, Price believed that 'the audience today is bigger, more awake, more eager for new vision, more receptive for change'

(1959: 230). His contemporary heroes were abstract expressionist painters like Mark Tobey, who had also inspired Shonberg (Chidester 2012). What Price admired in Tobey was the way in which he 'writes on his canvasses the language we all know so well, of hurry, speed, the ever changing glamour of the streets' (1959: 228). While he admired Tobey for expressing the feeling of modern life through colour, form and texture, he admired Richard Diebenkorn's abstract canvasses for the way in which they expressed 'the need to get away from reality' (1959: 231) in order to start anew. For Price these artists were visionaries, revolutionaries even, who stressed 'the possibility of change … not change for its own sake, but change for the sake of growth' (ibid.), spiritual growth. As an art connoisseur, devotee of abstract expressionism, impromptu poet and Poe aficionado, Price must have been delighted at the prospect of playing the visionary poet-artist-musician Roderick Usher. The role allowed him to unite his personal passions with those of the fictional character he portrayed, creating a figure charismatic in his eccentricity, of sensitive yet forceful personality, alienated by an unspeakable knowledge of his own and his sister's tragic fate that can be communicated only through the language of art. Roderick is a gothic abstract expressionist, whose notion of change is limited by visions of corruption and decay. As expressed by Roderick's painting in Poe's story: his soul is enclosed in darkness.

The first shot of Roderick is that of a man disturbed: 'what is the meaning of this?' (0:05:35), he exclaims in a low but disgruntled tone. During their first encounter, Philip and Roderick are contrasted through their dress, hairstyle and their position in the frame. Philip's pitch-black slick hairstyle cannot be more different to Roderick's white waves that come close to expressing the gossamer locks of Poe's original character. The two candles in the fore- and background divide the frame diagonally in two sections throwing up a boundary between Philip and Roderick, who is identified with the interior. The folds of his long red robe echo those of the drapery, and its colour matches that of the upholstery and the candles. The complete absence of any blue props make Philip the intruder in the frame. Throughout this opening confrontation, Roderick is presented as the sufferer, sitting down and winching at Philip's argumentative and forceful tone of voice.

Fig. 29 Suffering Roderick

Hendershot argues that Roderick represents abnormality in the film and claims that while he is 'a fascinating' villain he is 'scarcely sympathetic' (2000: 223). I believe, however, that the target audience of the film would have found it easier to identify with Roderick than with Philip, exactly because of his unconventional, hyper-sensitive, neurotic nature. As an angst-ridden and self-destructive personality, Roderick is much closer to a teenager than Philip, who in turn acts more like a parent. Moreover, when Roderick sits down to explain his affliction to Philip, he takes up the central position in the frame, holding his lute. Philip is out of shot, giving the impression that Roderick is addressing the audience.

Fig. 30 Melancholy Roderick

While he is not actually singing, his words are highly poetic, his tone velvet and melodious, his expressions revealing a melancholy resignation to his fate that invokes sympathy rather than antipathy:

> Madeline and I are life figures of fine glass. The slightest touch – and we may shatter. Both of us suffer from a morbid acuteness of the senses. Mine is the worst for having existed the longer – but both of us are afflicted with it. [brief pause] Any sort of food more exotic than the most pallid mash is unendurable to my taste buds. Any sort of garment other than the softest is agony to my flesh. My eyes are tormented by all but the faintest illumination. Odours assail me constantly, and as I've said, sounds of any degree whatsoever inspire me with terror … (0:10:13)

Then in an ominous whisper he says: 'I can hear the scratch of rat claws within the stone wall, Mr. Winthrop. Three-quarters of our family have fallen into madness. And in their madness have acquired a super-human strength so that it took the power of many to subdue them' (0:11:23). Price's Roderick displays his most vulnerable side to an uninvited guest (and the audience) in the poise of a minstrel confessing his innermost feelings.

When I watched the film for the first time, in 1990, the walls of my bedroom were adorned with posters of eccentric, sometimes effete, sometimes downright scary looking men with microphones and guitars (Alice Cooper, Twisted Sister, Queen). To my teenage brain, these 'weirdos' spoke the truth. Their words held more natural authority at the time than any parent or teacher, not because they were more rational or knowledgeable, but because their song lyrics and the melodrama of their music appealed to the emotional storm raging in my teenage mind. I can well imagine that in 1960 Roderick's minstrel persona had the potential to be understood as an allusion to the popular image of the dissident folk-singer.

Corman had been raised in California, where 'a vibrant left-wing folk scene' (Cohen 2002: 75) had developed in the post-war era, producing groups like The Gateway Singers, who, like The Weavers on the East Coast, 'combin[ed] Left politics and strong commercial aspirations' (Cohen 2002: 95). During the 50s, various folkies were investigated by the House Committee on Un-American Activities. Corman has described himself as a left-wing liberal and 'one of the older members of the counterculture' (Garris 2004). Throughout his AIP career he employed counterculture artists (e.g. Burt Shonberg, Country Joe and the Fish) and politically marginalised talents like Floyd Crosby (the father of singer-songwriters David and Ethan Crosby), who had been 'grey-listed'. What audiences at the time would not have known, probably, is that Price, like Crosby, 'had been greylisted' in the 1950s, and 'studios were advised not to use him' (Price 1999: 173). Victoria Price explains that after the success of *House of Wax*, her father's 'career suddenly and inexplicably appeared to stall' (1999: 172). Luckily, movie mavericks like Castle and Corman were all too willing to work with the unwanted and ignored, and the role of Roderick Usher would see Price back in the spotlight as an accomplished actor, rather than a ham-horror entertainer. What makes Roderick's angst hauntingly impressive is the way in which the Corman crew captured Roderick's posture and *mimique* as a sufferer, rather than a villain.

From the outset of his career Corman 'was attracted to stories about outcasts, misfits, or antiheroes on the run or on the fringe of society' (Corman 1998: 24). In *A Bucket of Blood* (1959), for instance, Corman satirised the bumptious tendencies of the Beat culture, but simultaneously painted a sympathetic portrait of youthful alienation and levelled critique at the commercialisation of art. The bohemian Yellow Door Café is transformed into a posh modern art gallery by its wheeler-dealer proprietor's corporate, rather than creative, talent. The film's tragic protagonist is the alienated and frustrated Walter Paisley, who works as a busboy at the Yellow Door but dreams of being an artist. His desire to be recognised by his peers leads him into a misguided and macabre attempt to reach the limelight by covering corpses in clay. After Paisley has created his first cadaver statue, an unassuming folk musician at the Yellow Door functions as a Greek chorus of sorts (the same role played by the character Poe on his chopper in *Gas-s-s-s*). He expresses to the audience what Walter cannot acknowledge: 'Go down, you murderer, go down' (0:28:28). The singer is none other than Alex Hassilev, who would go on to form the Limeliters with one of California's most radical folkies, Lou Gottlieb. In *A Bucket of Blood*, Corman juxtaposes false and true forms of art. False art is created for the wrong reasons: public attention, high social standing and financial gain, values prized by the mainstream. True works of art, like the folk-singer's songs, are honest expressions of experience and feeling. Roderick Usher, like Walter Paisley, may have lost the plot entirely, but his artworks, like Walter's, are expressive of the mental anguish that has led him astray. Harold Hildebrand, writing in the *LA Examiner* on 17 July 1960, understood Price's vision of Roderick when he wrote 'although you will be shocked by his deeds in *House of Usher*, you nonetheless feel compassion for the distorted reasoning behind them' (qtd in Williams 1998: 164). In opening up to Philip, Roderick may be displaying the unbalanced state of his mind, but Philip's unsympathethic response: 'Do you not exaggerate sir; perhaps there have been in your family certain … peculiarities of temperament' (0:11:45), puts him in the position of antagonist. Corman has argued that he 'felt the audience shouldn't be afraid of Roderick Usher based on any sinister features or brute strength … If you were afraid of him, it would be on the basis of his superior mental qualities' (French 2007: 44). Price's soft-spoken yet tormented tone during his initial confrontation with Philip, and Philip's incredulous response, invite the predominantly adolescent audience to take Roderick's side. Roderick shares the adolescent audience's openness to wonder and fragility to fright. Philip, in his condescending rationality, performs the role of the incredulous parent. Roderick resembles Jim Stark more than he does Norman Bates.

Fig. 31 A Bucket of Blood

The dramatic tension developed between Roderick and Philip in the course of the plot encourages the presumed adolescent audience to sympathise with Price's artistic misfit, despite the increasingly unhinged state of his mind and his elderly appearance. Price has explained: 'what I wanted to do was give the impression that Roderick had never been outside of that house, or even seen the sun. So you'd get the impression that he has spent his whole life locked up in that house' (qtd in French 2007: 41). This sense of imprisonment in the family home must have struck a chord with adolescent audiences who were probably at the cinema to get away from their parents. The daily life experienced by Roderick would be the very nightmare future scenario teenagers would be dreading: a life of 24/7 domestic imprisonment brought about by the wrongs of the fathers. In teenage terms, Roderick has been grounded indefinitely, which must make him sympathetic. Victoria Price explains that her father indeed intended to play Roderick as a victim:

> With his white hair, pale skin, and pale blue eyes, he looked almost albino, as if the cursed place and tainted line of the House of Usher had stripped him of life itself. As the tortured and sensitive Roderick, Price delivered a restrained performance in the role of the cursed brother who tries to protect his sister and her suitor from the inevitable consequences of their ancestry. (1999: 212)

Corman too has stressed that Roderick is not the villain of the story. In his perspective of the story, Roderick does not deny Madeline her happiness because it is his patriarchal duty to ensure she marries a man whose wealth and power will benefit the Usher lineage. Rather, 'Usher won't let [Philip and Madeline] marry for fear of spreading their dreaded hereditary madness' (Corman 1998: 78), a madness – the Usher portraits illustrate – that has led countless ancestors into evil ways, bringing pain and suffering on many others. His motive is altruistic, no matter how misguided. By killing off the Usher family, Roderick symbolically rejects concepts such as historical tradition, deference to parental authority and the institution of the nuclear family, which had been 'the bedrock of democracy and capitalism, freedom and prosperity, security and stability' in the 1950s (Cohen 2002: 96).

Fig. 32 Rebel Without a Cause

Fig. 33 Roderick's despair

Vincent Price's facial expressions and body language are the true vehicles for the expression of emotion in the film, just like James Dean's in *Rebel Without a Cause* (1955). Like Dean, Price is able to establish a non-verbal communication channel with the audience that overrides the other characters' reasoning. Just as Jim Stark's parents' arguments do little more than evoke resistance in the youthful part of the audience, Philip Winthrop's stubborn insistence on taking Madeline away evokes antipathy, rather than understanding. Roderick is candid about his family's past, his and Madeline's present reality, and their dismal future. His distraught gaze in response to Philip's command –

'She leaves with me today!' (0:42:31) – leaves no doubt about the depth of his despair.
Roderick's reasoning may prove unsound, but his feelings are genuine. He is convinced
that his doom is 'my birthright and my curse' (0:22:08), to borrow Nicholas Medina's
words in *The Pit and the Pendulum*. Roderick is eventually manhandled by a desparate
Philip whose frustration boils over into a violent passion to 'rescue' Madeline from her
brother's (and the House's) influence.

Figs. 34–35 Philip's aggression

This confrontation could have put Roderick in a bad light had the Corman crew brought
Philip's passion into focus. Instead, the frames are composed and lit to foreground
Roderick's helplessness and suffering at the hands of the younger man. What is more,
Philip's thrashing about the house proves pointless and the subsequent dream sequence
reveals that he thinks of Roderick as a rival to be defeated, rather than a neurotic to be
appeased. Roderick's malignly sneering visage in the dream needs to be understood as a
personification of Philip's understanding of his character. The vast difference between the
sensitive sufferer in the house and the arrogant, mocking figure in the dream leaves little
doubt as to which of the two is the genuine character of Roderick.

The final confrontation between Roderick and Philip finds Usher again sitting down
with his lute, surrounded by various artistic impliments. While Philip expresses his desire
to kill Roderick in revenge for murdering his sister, the camera moves to face Roderick
while he explains: 'You will never understand; to so logical a mind as yours I have

committed murder. If you only knew the agonies I have spared you and the world. If you only knew the agonies I have endured on your behalf' (1:02:57). Roderick's explanation here fits his characterisation as developed by Matheson and Corman. *House of Usher* is a gothic fantasy, not a realistic teen drama like *Rebel Without a Cause*.

Fig. 36 Roderick's agony

To properly understand Roderick Usher you need to accept the supernatural premise that underlies the plot. The film's hero is convinced he has inherited his ancestor's evil and has decided that the only way to save the world from the Ushers is to destroy their world entirely, which tragically includes his sister. To a rational human being who rejects the possibility of inherited evil, like Philip, Usher's reasoning, like Jim Stark's reasoning about being called a chicken, is highly irrational and destructive. But what made Jim Stark such a charismatic if controversial hero was his rejection of ideologically prescribed social roles and individual identities. He hated his parents for their blind conformity to the status quo, but equally rejected the alternative codes of the greaser subculture, making him a total outsider. *Rebel Without a Cause* is ultimately a mainstream melodrama that simultaneously addresses the problems of youthful alienation, but seeks to solve this problem conventionally by rewarding its anti-hero with a girlfriend and a reconciliation with his parents by the end. For all intents and purposes, Jim Stark has been absorbed into the fold of normality when the credits roll. Roderick Usher, by contrast, is a Romantic hero trapped in an apocalyptic fantasy. His own and his sister's demise are preordained as the plot demands a catastrophe. Roderick is finally confronted with what he always feared was to be his fate, death at the hands of his family. This may not be a realistic ending, but then, the film is a fantasy. The catastrophe perfectly fits its gothic theme of the sins of the fathers being visited upon the next generation. Roderick's angst proves to be not a sign of madness, but of foresight.

ANGER: MYRNA FAHEY'S MADELINE

In Poe's story Madeline appears only once, fleetingly, in the shadows of Roderick's gloomy chamber, before being buried in the family vault. In her second and final appearance during the catastrophe, she reappears bloody, emaciated, 'trembling and reeling to and fro upon the threshold' before falling 'heavily inward upon the person of her brother, and in her violent and now final death-agonies' bearing 'him to the floor a corpse, and a victim to the terrors he had anticipated' (2000: 416-17). Poe's Madeline is a symbolic figure, remaining entirely undescribed by the narrator, apart from his observation that 'the face of the tenant' – the body in the coffin – bore 'a striking similitude' (2000: 410) to Roderick. On the one hand, this implies that the siblings are twins. On the other hand, the allegorical structure of the story suggests that the figures that flit through the shadows of Roderick's chamber and disappear behind doors, like Madeline, represent aspects of Roderick's psyche which he fears to acknowledge, but knows he must confront. Therefore, the face in the coffin is more likely to be a projection of Roderick's own psyche. Madeline is the death he longs for, but which he simultaneously fears, as his mystical studies have done little to fill the black void he suspects awaits him on his dissolution.

Karl S. Guthke explains that during the nineteenth century, in contrast to the masculine world of empire, industry and culture, artists came to perceive an 'intimate connection of the female sex with the "elemental", with "nature", or biological processes' (1999: 189). Significantly, as the hegemonic masculine ideology equated reason and science with progress, feminine nature, with its endless cycles of life, death and rebirth, came to be negatively associated with corruption and decay. By the end of the century, Guthke explains, various artists produced works that utilised the classical myth of the avenging Furies to give expression to anxieties over the repression and exploitation of woman/nature by men/science. Not only was the *fin-de-siècle* Fury 'a goddess of revenge' who 'inflicts death', she even came 'to stand for it, indeed to embody' death (1999: 190). In 'The Fall of the House of Usher', Madeline becomes such an avenging fury at the catastrophe, a symbol of the inevitable decay of all that nature can create.

Fig. 37 Madeline

In contrast to Poe's symbolic figure, Myrna Fahey's Madeline is a 'real' person with a real presence in the film. She is an individual human being with her own hopes, fears and desires. Rather than haunting the distant corners of Roderick's mind, Fahey's Madeline enters the frame centre-screen, interrupting her brother's conversation with Philip and demanding that her fiancé be allowed to stay. Her introduction in the film follows Matheson's characterisation of her as 'a beautiful and willful woman in her early twenties' who had known a life outside the House of Usher, in Boston, where she had met and fallen in love with Philip Winthrop. However, Matheson adds that having 'accepted [Roderick's] beliefs regarding the house' she has returned 'to live – and die' there, only for the appearance of Philip to give her 'new hope that, perhaps, Roderick is wrong and it is not necessary that she perish with the house' (French 2007: 51-2). The fact that Madeline's engagement to Philip is not known to Roderick underscores her wilfulness. She is clearly capable of keeping a secret from her brother, i.e. one that – from his perspective – could lead to the perpetuation of the Usher evil for another generation. Apart from successfully demanding that Philip stays, Madeline also successfully challenges her brother at dinner, underscoring that she is not entirely passive and helpless, even if she labours under the great strain of the family illness in which both Roderick and Madeline believe.

According to Hendershot, *House of Usher* is ultimately about the male abuse of patriarchal power. She argues that 'Roderick's vehement objection to Philip is over the issue of marriage' and that 'Madeline wants to leave with Philip, but Roderick pressures her to stay' (2000: 223). But Roderick's reasons for rejecting the marriage, no matter how marvellous, are clearly stated at the outset of the film and do not suggest a will to patriarchal power on his part. After having explained the nature of the Usher evil to Philip, Roderick explains further, when Madeline has supposedly passed away, that 'mere passage from the flesh cannot undo centuries of evil. There can be no peace without penalty … I did not wish her death. I only knew that it was inevitable – as my death is inevitable. Our blight must be removed from this Earth' (0:47:46). This is what Roderick believes and what motivates his rejection of Philip's demands to take Madeline away from the House.

Earlier in the film, Madeline explained to Philip why she could not leave the house even if she wanted to: 'very soon I shall be dead' (0:31:34). As in his confrontations with Roderick, Philip tries to impress his notions on Madeline: 'I forbid you to say that ever again … you're full of life' (0:31:40). Like Roderick, Madeline replies: 'I wish you could understand' (0:32:03). Both Roderick and Madeline perceive themselves as tragic victims of a family curse and Madeline is determined to show Philip the truth in the vault: 'Perhaps you'll feel differently after you've seen' (0:32:17). When she guides Philip into the family vault to show him the caskets of her grandparents and parents she also shows him her own coffin – 'it waits for me' (0:35:36) – and explains that there is one for Roderick as well. The Usher siblings firmly believe in their mutual fate and hope that for Philip seeing will be believing.

House of Usher is a fantastic film. Its plot, like Hammer's *Dracula* and *Frankenstein*, revolves around a fantastic premise, in this case the classic gothic trope of the sins of the fathers living on to curse generation after generation. To take the film seriously, one has to approach it on its own terms as a gothic story and accept this fantastic premise. Matheson's characterisations are designed around this motif, and, as in Hawthorne's *The House of the Seven Gables*, are specifically designed to reveal one generation of siblings struggling to overcome the evil grip of their ancestors. Roderick and Madeline, each in their own way rebel against the past, as each attempts to alter their destiny. But as Roderick's visionary art foreshadows, their victory will come at the cost of their total dissolution.

Aleksandrowicz has a point when he claims that 'strong and positive females are scarce in Corman's gothic horrors' (2016: 160). But it is important to recognise that strong and positive males, in the traditional sense of masculinity, are equally absent from these films. Roderick Usher is a visionary artist who has foreseen his fate and has become obsessed with ending the family curse before it is too late. Nicholas Medina, in *The Pit and the Pendulum*, is a cuckolded milksop at the mercy of his wife's and his physician's desires.

Premature Burial's Guy Carrell, played by Ray Milland, is probably the most Poesque of all Corman's protagonists, hopelessly obsessed with thoughts of death and equally fearful of the afterlife, as his paintings (also by Shonberg) indicate. In this film, Hazel Court, playing Carrell's beloved Emily Gault, is the strongest character, not because she is more rational than Guy, but because she shows a strong personality by trying to understand and alleviate Guy's suffering.

In terms of representing individual men and women on the screen, Corman avoided stereotypes that embodied constrictive traditional values. His best pictures present a morally ambiguous world in which neither conventional men nor conventional women hold the high ground, but in which strong individual personalities survive in times of adversity. Beverly Garland plays several strong characters who battle injustice, invasion and prejudice, especially in *Not of this Earth*, in which her character shows more agency than any other. By contrast, Charles Bronson's George 'Machine Gun' Kelly is a moral coward hiding behind a false front of machismo and male aggression. His lover, Florence 'Flo' Becker, played by Susan Cabot, turns out to be the cold-hearted criminal mastermind behind their success. When the criminal gang gets its comeuppance, all that Kelly can say is, 'I didn't want any part of it Flo, it was all your fault' (1:22:30). Kelly may be the protagonist of the picture, but he is not a hero. Neither is Flo the picture's heroine, in the traditional sense. The film is a psychological study of the making of a criminal. It is not interested in pointing a moral finger, but in trying to understand its characters' perspectives on life and the motivations for their criminal actions.

House of Usher is similarly a film that explores character motivation rather than conventional morality. Convinced of their family's evil heritage and their evil inheritance, Roderick and Madeline carry a heavy burden. Following social conventions by marrying and continuing the family line will perpetuate the Usher evil. This knowledge does not stop Madeline from desiring Philip, however, because rejecting social conventions, she knows, will mean ostracisation from society, followed by a period of physical and mental suffering she can share only with her brother, and inevitable death. Unsurprisingly, Madeline, the younger of the two siblings – and according to Roderick not as deeply stricken with the Usher illness as himself – finds in the appearance of Philip a chance of escape. 'My life is my own' (0:20:53) she exclaims, defying her brother: 'Do you hate me so you wish to keep me prisoner here?' (0:21:03). She loves Philip, and desires to rebel against her ancestral fate. But as Bristol explains to Philip, Madeline 'is obsessed by thoughts of death' (0:26:56), illustrated by her sleep-walking journey to the chapel, where she lies on the altar, as if dead.

 Matheson's script allowed Madeline only to demand: 'I will be free!' (French 2007: 127). The filmed scene contains quite lengthy dialogue between Roderick and Madeline in which only Madeline's words are audible. Her words, when isolated, make wonderful lyrics for a feminist pop-song:

No, Roderick
No, I will not listen
I've been here long enough
Please let me go
(Louder) I don't care what you say
you can't keep me here
No, no, Roderick
No I will not listen
please let me go
there may be no hope for you, but there is for me
(Louder) I say I will
I must leave, Roderick
Please let me go
(Louder) I don't care what you say
There's nothing you can say to me, Roderick
I will leave! (0:41:13)

Corman has stressed that he believed in the feminist movement (1998: 34). In the 1950s, one of the aims of the feminist movement he believed worthwhile supporting was the need for the female voice to be heard more loudly in society. Sometimes Corman's approach to this issue is rather heavy-handed, if well-meaning, as in *Teenage Doll* (1957), starring June Kenney as Barbara Bonney, a female Jim Stark. In other films his interest in presenting independent women with an individual voice is more subtle, as in *Not of this Earth*. The voice of Myrna Fahey's Madeline Usher is similarly subtle in expressing itself against tradition. On the one hand, you could argue that Madeline's

Figs. 38–39 Madeline's fury

plea to be heard is silenced in the film because she is buried alive, itself an allegorical representation of women's voice in society. You could also argue that Madeline stands in an inferior position to her brother by pointing out that in her struggle she is pleading with Roderick ('please let me go'). On the other hand, you could foreground her independence by counting the times she denies her brother's words; her negations definitely outnumber her pleas. Above all, Madeline's voice is loudest in exclaiming 'I don't care' and 'I will', phrases expressive of the strength of her determination to do her own thing. During the crucial argument between Roderick and Madeline, it is Roderick's voice that goes unheard. And while it is true that Madeline fails to leave the house with Philip, what exactly happens that puts her into a catatonic state remains unclear. Philip accuses Roderick of murder, for he does not believe in the Usher curse, but as discussed in chapter two, the viewer has to decide for him or herself which of the two perspectives of the story to believe: Philip's or Roderick's. It is a testament to Matheson's skill as a script writer that he was able to give Madeline an individual personality that simultaneously believes in, yet rebels against her fate, without betraying Poe's concept that Madeline and Roderick were united by their mutual relation to the house.

Poe's original story gave Matheson and Corman the opportunity – or I should say forced Matheson and Corman – to resurrect Madeline at the climax of the film so that she could fulfil her own and her brother's destiny. In her sudden appearance, the representation of her resembles that of Roderick's painting very closely. Significantly, at the catastrophe only Madeline has any agency left. She has adopted the role of avenging Fury unambiguously. Roderick, fearful of her strength, only cowers at her sudden appearance in his chamber and Philip is dragged away by Bristol. The final scene is an antiparallel to the opening scene in which Madeline first appears. Madeline again appears suddenly and unannounced, but now it is she who forcefully embraces her brother, not to comfort him, but to fulfil his own prophecy and to exact revenge for Roderick's act of sororicide. The final close-up of Madeline leaves no doubt which of the two Usher spirits was the strongest. After the house goes up in flames, the final line of Poe's story [slightly misquoted] appears in the final frame of Corman's film before the end credits, informing the viewer that 'the deep and dank tarn closed silently over the fragments of the House of Usher' (1:14:12).

Conclusion: The Genre of *Usher*

Poe's 'The Fall of the House of Usher' has been adapted for the screen many times. Certain versions, like Jean Epstein's 1928 silent film, are stylish productions, faithful to the spirit, if not the letter of the original. Others, like the curious GIB Films production of 1950, the wayward 1979 TV movie, starring Martin Landau, and the preposterous 1989 film starring Oliver Reed, take such liberties with the plot and characters of the story that they should be understood as re-imaginings of Poe, rather than screen adaptions of a literary source. It is an often repeated piece of apocrypha that Roger Corman sold his version of *House of Usher* to AIP by assuring them that 'the house is the monster' (French 2007: 24). In his memoir, Corman stresses that he delivered on this unique selling point (1998: 79). But is *House of Usher* really a monster movie?

From my analysis I have to conclude that there is little truly monstrous about the mansion itself, in the way that Shirley Jackson's Hill House or Stephen King's Rose Red are truly alive and evil. Rather than creating a monstrous mansion, I would say that the Corman crew successfully recast the fulcrum of Poe's story, the allegorical ballad titled 'The Haunted Palace', into a cinematic set. The house that Daniel Haller built is an extended metaphor for Roderick's mind, the tenor of which is the state of Roderick and Madeline's souls imprisoned in their mansion. But as chapter four showed, Madeline is no longer simply a projection of Roderick's psyche, as she is in Poe's tale. This is not how audiences in 1960 would have understood her character. She is too much present in body and voice to be considered merely a symbolic figure. Therefore, it is better to categorise *House of Usher* – if categorise we must – as a film belonging to a subgenre of haunted-house narratives identified by Barry Curtis as revolving around 'tragic families and the influence of the past on the present' (2008: 16). Such films are 'parables of thwarted and demented domesticity … warning against succumbing to a binding relationship between person and place that might continue after death' (2008: 43).

House of Usher is a fantastic tale; the bond between Roderick, Madeline and their family mansion is made very clear in the course of the film. But is it really possible to speak of the House of Usher as haunted? Does the film concern the possession of the house, and thus also Roderick and Madeline's souls, by a ghost that needs to be exorcised, as in Hollywood's greatest ghost story, *The Uninvited* (1944)? In contrast to

Poe's narrator, Philip Winthrop is indeed uninvited and is presented with an insoluble mystery that Roderick calls a family curse. But Roderick and Madeline are only haunted metaphorically by their knowledge of the family evil. Their ancestors do not float about the corridors in white robes, clanging their chains to shock intruders. Roderick is 'haunted' by the evil deeds of his ancestors because their horrific and unlawful actions have tainted the family name, and according to Roderick, have literally infected the environment and the very atmosphere he breathes, like a nefarious mildew. He is suffering the consequences of their crimes.

As a film set in an old, dark house, inhabited by a family harbouring secrets, which are uncovered by a spirited outsider, *House of Usher* bears some resemblance to the 'Old Dark House' genre to which James Whale's 1932 classic gave its name. Whale's original is famous for its exquisite balance of black humour and moments of true horror, as well as its atmospheric cinematography. Following the success of *The Old Dark House*, high-spirited pseudo-gothic pictures featuring heroic dandies, damsels in distress, outlandish villains and happy endings became standard fare for Universal, from *The House of the Seven Gables* (1940) to *The Strange Door* (1951) and *The Black Castle* (1952). While Corman had successfully dabbled in the black comedy genre with the satirical *A Bucket of Blood* and the potty *Little Shop of Horrors* (1960), *House of Usher* lacks the biting wit of these two pictures, or the swashbuckling romance of Universal's gothics. Above all, there is no happy ending for Roderick, Madeline, Philip or even Bristol. From the outset of the film, doom and gloom persist and total collapse proves inevitable as the flaming house sinks into the tarn. It is this lack of a traditional denouement that distinguishes *House of Usher* (as well as *Premature Burial*) from the films that it most directly resembles in terms of production values and acting performances: Hammer's *Curse of Frankenstein* and *Horror of Dracula*.

So *House of Usher* is not a monster movie, nor an 'old-dark-house' picture. While it definitely falls into the genre of nineteenth-century gothic adaptations fashionable in Britain and America from the early 30s to the late 60s, Poe's claustrophobic allegory is a literary source that only in the broadest sense dovetails with novels like *Frankenstein*, *Dracula* or *Strange Case of Dr. Jekyll and Mr. Hyde*. In contrast to the Universal and Hammer adaptations of these literary classics, Corman's *House of Usher* contains neither a gothic monster nor a villain; there is definitely a damsel in distress, but then *everyone* in the film is in distress. The romantic lead is rather dull and his increasing bewilderment makes him the most ineffectual of heroes. Moreover, the most charismatic figure in the film, and the protagonist who evokes the most sympathy from the viewer, is an isolated neurotic artist convinced that only his and his sister's death will rid the world of 'a plague of evil'. As such, *House of Usher* is uncategorisable in its complexity as a genre picture. It foregrounds Usher's role as an outsider, the last of the family line who has rejected the vicious life of his ancestors but suffers from a crippling sense of guilt for the crimes they have committed. His sensitivity and artistic temperament allow him to express through painting and music alone what he cannot express in words: a feeling of utter dread at the thought of the older generations prolonging their evil sway over the next generation and a deeply felt desire fraught with fear to witness the end of it all. Commercially, *House of Usher* was AIP's answer to Hammer; thematically, *House of Usher* looks forward to *Gas-s-s-s, or It Became Necessary to Destroy the World in Order to Save It!* Both are angst-ridden apocalyptic features aimed at teenagers living through genuinely apocalyptic times.

Bibliography / Filmography

Aleksandrowicz, Pawel. *The Cinematography of Roger Corman: Exploitation Filmmaker or Auteur?* Newcastle: Cambridge Scholars Publishing, 2016.

Alfonso, Barry. 'Burt Shonberg Biography'. 2015. Burtshonberg.com. Consulted on 26 June 2017.

Allen, Lewis (dir). *The Uninvited*. Paramount, 1944. Exposure Cinema DVD.

'American International Pictures Retrospective at the Museum of Modern Art'. *MoMA Press Release*, No. 47 (July 1979).

Arkoff, Samuel Z. 'The Guardian Lecture'. 11 August 1991. On *The Undead*. Dir. Roger Corman. American International Pictures. The Arkoff Film Library. Direct Video DVD.

Barnett, Ivan (dir). *The Fall of the House of Usher*. GIB, 1950. Renown DVD.

Bassie, Ashley. *Expressionism*. New York: Parkstone, 2008.

Bauer, John I.H. *Revolution and Tradition: An Exhibition of the Chief Movements in American Painting from 1900 to the Present*. NY: Brooklyn Museum Press, 1951.

Baxley, Craig R (dir). *Stephen King's Rose Red*. Victor Television Production, 2001. Warner Bros. DVD.

'BFI Interview with Roger Corman'. 2013. Youtube.com. Consulted on 2 June 2016.

Bible, The. Oxford: Oxford World's Classics, 1997.

Birkinshaw, Alan (dir). *The House of Usher*. Youtube.com. Consulted on 15 January 2017.

Bourke, Joanna. *Fear: A Cultural History*. London: Virago, 2005.

Brahm, John (dir). *The Mad Magician*. Columbia, 1954. Savoy DVD.

Burgers, Jan W.J. *The Lute in the Dutch Golden Age*. Amsterdam: Amsterdam University Press, 2013.

Burke, Edmund. *A Philosophical Enquiry into the Origin of our Ideas of the Sublime and Beautiful*. Oxford: Oxford World's Classics, 2008.

Chidester, Brian. 'A Declaration of Independents'. 2012. Burtshonberg.com. Consulted on 26 June 2017.

Cohen, Ronald D. *Rainbow Quest: The Folk Music Revival & American Society, 1940-1970*. Amherst: University of Massachusetts Press, 2002.

Conway, James L (dir). *Usherin Kirous* [*The Fall of the House of Usher*]. Sun Classic Pictures, 1979. Alfa Panorama Film & Video VHS.

Corman, Roger, with Jim Jerome. *How I Made A Hundred Movies in Hollywood and Never Lost a Dime*. New York: Da Capo Press, 1998.

--- (dir). *Day the World Ended*. American International Pictures, 1956. Direct Video DVD.

--- (dir). *Attack of the Crab Monsters*. American International Pictures, 1956. IN2FILM DVD.

--- (dir). *Not of this Earth*. American International Pictures, 1956. IN2FILM DVD.

--- (dir). *War of the Satellites*. American International Pictures, 1958. Youtube.com

--- (dir). *Machine Gun Kelly*. American International Pictures, 1958. Youtube.com

--- (dir). *A Bucket of Blood*. American International Pictures, 1959. Dripping Blood DVD.

--- (dir). *House of Usher*. American International Pictures, 1960. MGM DVD.

--- (dir). *Pit and the Pendulum*. American International Pictures, 1961. MGM DVD.

--- (dir). *Creature from the Haunted Sea*. American International Pictures, 1961. Bach Films DVD.

--- (dir). *Premature Burial*. American International Pictures, 1962. Green Cow DVD.

--- (dir). *Gas-s-s-s, or It Became Necessary to Destroy the World in Order to Save It!* MGM American International Pictures, 1970. MGM DVD.

Curtis, Barry. *Dark Places: The Haunted House in Film*. London: Reaktion, 2008.

Dixon, Wheeler Winston. 'Floyd Crosby, ASC – The Great Cinematographers'. *Frame by Frame*, University of Nebraska-Lincoln. http://blog.unl.edu/dixon/. Consulted on 18 July 2017.

Doherty, Thomas. *Teenagers and Teenpics: The Juvenilization of American Movies in the 1950s*. Philadelphia: Temple University Press, 2002.

Epstein, Jean (dir). *The Fall of the House of Usher*. 1928. Youtube.com. Consulted on 11 May 2017.

Frank, Alan. *The Films of Roger Corman: 'Shooting My Way out of Trouble'*. London: Batsford: 1998.

French, Lawrence, ed. *Visions of Death: Richard Matheson's Edgar Allan Poe Scripts, Volume 1*. Colorado Springs: Gauntlet Press, 2007.

Furst, Lilian R. 'The Romantic Hero, Or Is He an Anti-hero?' *Studies in the Literary Imagination* 9.1 (1976): 53-67.

Garris, Mick. 'Post-Mortem: Roger Corman'. 2014. *Mick Garris Interviews*. Youtube.com. Consulted on 2 June 2016.

Goodman, Paul. *Growing Up Absurd*. New York: Vintage, 1960.

Günther, Winfried. 'Der Untergang Des Hauses Usher'. *Retro Filmprogramm 20* (oktober 1982): n.p.

Guthke, Karl S. *The Gender of Death: A Cultural History in Art and Literature*. Cambridge: Cambridge University Press, 1999.

Hadfield, J.A. *Dreams and Nightmares*. Harmondsworth: Penguin, 1954.

Heffernan, Kevin. *Ghouls, Gimmicks, and Gold: Horror Films and the American Movie Business, 1953-1968*. Durham: Duke University Press, 2004.

Heller, Terry. *The Delights of Terror: An Aesthetics of the Tale of Terror*. Urbana: University of Illinois Press, 1987.

Hendershot, Cyndy. 'Domesticity and Horror in *House of Usher* and *Village of the Damned*'. *Quarterly Review of Film and Video* 17.3 (2000): 221-227.

'House of Usher' (1960). *National Film Registry*. www.loc.gov/programs/national-film-preservation-board/film-registry/complete-national-film-registry-listing/ descriptions-and-essays/. Consulted on 14 March 2016.

IJdelheid Der IJdelheden: Hollandse Vanitas-Voorstellingen Uit de Zeventiende Eeuw. Leiden: Lakenhal, 1970.

Jancovich, Mark. *Rational Fears: American Horror in the 1950s*. Manchester: Manchester University Press, 1996.

Jackson, Shirley. *The Haunting [of Hill House]*. London: Penguin, 1999.

Jones, Barbara. *Follies & Grottoes*. London: Constable, 1974.

Juran, Nathan (dir). *The Black Castle*. Universal International, 1952. L'Atelier 13 DVD.

Kansa, Spencer. *Out There: The Transcendent Life and Art of Burt Shonberg*. Oxford: Mandrake, 2017.

King, Stephen. *On Writing*. London: Hodder, 2000.

Kouwer, B.J. *Colors and their Character: A Psychological Study*. The Hague: Martinus Nijhoff, 1949.

Levin, Harry. *The Power of Blackness*. London: faber & faber, 1958.

Leiber, Fritz. 'The Conjure Wife'. *Unknown* (April 1943): 9-78.

Lucas, Tim. 'Interview with Roger Corman at the Hi-Pointe Theatre in St. Louis on Saturday, May 21, 2011'. Youtube.com. Consulted on 12 June 2017.

Matheson, Richard. 'Mad House' (1953). In *Nightmare at 20.000 Feet*. New York: Tor, 2002. 67-105.

Mokre, Jan. 'The Symbolism of the Globe – Past and Present'. Lecture given on 24 October 2000 at the Osher Map Library, Portland, Maine, USA. www.academia.edu/14735863/The Symbolism of the Globe Past and Present. Consutled on 25 July 2017.

Morris, Gary. 'From the House to the Tomb: Exploring the Corman/Poe Films'. *Bright Lights Film Journal* (October 2010), n.p. Brightlightsfilm.com. Consulted on 28 February 2017.

National Film Preservation Board. https://www.loc.gov/programs/national-film-preservation-board/film-registry/complete-national-film-registry-listing/. Consulted on 28 July 2017.

Naha, Ed. *The Films of Roger Corman: Brilliance on a Budget*. New York: Arco, 1982.

Ostrom, John Ward, ed. *The Letters of Edgar Allan Poe*. 2 volumes. Cambridge: Harvard University Press, 1948.

Perry, Dennis R and Carl H. Sederholm, eds. *Adapting Poe: Re-Imaginings in Popular Culture*. London: Palgrave, 2012.

Pevney, Joseph (dir). *The Strange Door*. Universal International, 1951. L'Atelier 13 DVD.

Poe, Edgar Allan. *Essays and Reviews*. Ed. G.R. Thompson. New York: Library of America, 1984.

---. 'The Fall of the House of Usher'. In *Tales and Sketches, Volume 1: 1831-1842*. Ed. Thomas Ollive Mabbott. Urbana: University of Illinois Press, 2000. 392-421.

---. *Complete Poems*. Ed. Thomas Ollive Mabbott. Urbana: University of Illinois Press, 2000.

Preston, Ward. *What an Art Director Does: An Introduction to Motion Picture Production Design*. Los Angeles: Silman James Press, 1994.

Price, Victoria. *Vincent Price: A Daughter's Biography*. New York: St. Martin's Press, 1999.

Price, Vincent. *I Like What I Know: A Visual Autobiography*. Garden City: Doubleday, 1959.

---, and V.B. Price. *Monsters*. New York: Grosset & Dunlap, 1981.

 'Psychedelische Poe'. *NRC* (30 May 2001): n.p. http://vorige.nrc.nl/krant/article1535227.ece. Consulted on 13 August 2015.

Quinn, Arthur Hobson. *Edgar Allan Poe*. Baltimore: Johns Hopkins University Press, 1998.

Ray, Nicholas (dir). *Rebel Without a Cause*. Warner Bros. 1955. Warner Bros. DVD.

Schenk, H.G. *The Mind of the European Romantics*. London: Constable, 1966.

Sharrett, Christopher. 'Corman's Poe and Male Hysteria in 60s Horror: A Revaluation'. *Film International* (October 2012), n.p.

Shonberg, Burt, with Ledru Shoopman Baker III. 'Out Here'. 2009. Burtshonberg.com Consulted on 4 May 2017.

Silverman, Kenneth. *Edgar A. Poe*. New York: HarperCollins, 1991.

Skal, David J. *The Monster Show: A Cultural History of Horror*. London: Plexus, 1994.

Swedenborg, Emanuel. *Heaven and Hell*. 1758. Trans. John C. Anger. West Chester: Swedenborg Foundation, 1995.

Tudor, Andrew. *Monsters and Mad Scientists: A Cultural History of the Horror Movie*. Oxford: Blackwell, 1989.

'The Curse of Harkley Heath'. *Vault of Horror* 13 (1950). Archive.org. Consulted on 12 June 2017.

Van Leeuwen, Evert Jan. 'Hero of Horror: Edgar Allan Poe (1809-1849)'. In *Celebrity Authorship and Afterlives in English and American Literature*. Eds. Gaston Franssen and Rick Honings. London: Palgrave, 2016. 43-66.

---. *Poetic Meditations on Death: A Gothic and Romantic Literary Genre of the Long Eighteenth Century 1693-1858*. Lewiston: EMP, 2014.

Vaughan, William, et.al. *Caspar David Friedrich 1774-1840*. London: Tate Gallery, 1972.

Versluis, Arthur, *The Esoteric Origins of the American Renaissance*. Oxford: Oxford University Press, 2001.

Whale John (dir). *The Old Dark House*. Universal, 1932. Network DVD.

Whittington, Karl. 'Caspar David Friedrich's Medieval Burials'. *Nineteenth-Century Art Worldwide* 11.1 (Spring 2012): n.p. http://www.19thc-artworldwide.org/spring12/Whittington-on-caspar-david-friedrichs-medieval-burials. Consulted on 13 April 2017.

Wilbur, Richard. 'The House of Poe'. In *The Recognition of Edgar Allan Poe: Selected Criticism Since 1829*. Ed. Eric W. Carlson. Ann Arbor: University of Michigan Press, 1966. 255-77.

Williams, Lucy Chase. *The Complete Films of Vincent Price*. Secaucus: Citadel Press, 1998.

Wright, Bruce Lanier. *Nightwalkers: Gothic Horror Movies – The Modern Era*. Dallas: Taylor, 1995.

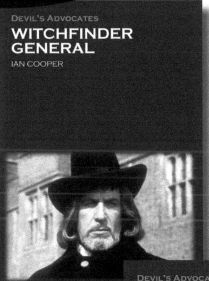

DEVIL'S ADVOCATES
WITCHFINDER GENERAL
IAN COOPER

"...one of the best books on film I've ever read... Cooper writes with clarity, wit and confidence, his obvious fondness for the film and for movies in general evident throughout..."
Horror Talk

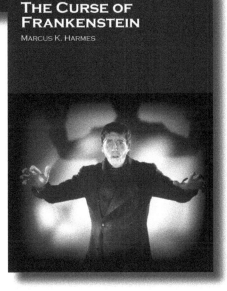

DEVIL'S ADVOCATES
THE CURSE OF FRANKENSTEIN
MARCUS K. HARMES

"...the biggest strength of Harmes' writing is successfully finding fresh angles... Concise and easy to digest in a single sitting, it adds up to a delicious read for Hammer fans."
Frightfest.co.uk

Milton Keynes UK
Ingram Content Group UK Ltd.
UKHW020638090624
443798UK00010B/172